A GUIDE FOR WOMEN

Using the Twelve Steps
to Grow Spiritually

A GUIDE FOR WOMEN

Using the Twelve Steps
to Grow Spiritually

BY

Patricia F. Wallace, M.A.

and

Sister Mary Winifred, C.H.S., M.A.

AN AUTHORS GUILD BACKINPRINT.COM EDITION

A Guide for Women
Using the Twelve Steps to Grow Spiritually
All Rights Reserved © 1992, 2000 by Patricia F. Wallace and Mary Winifred

AN AUTHORS GUILD BACKINPRINT.COM EDITION

Published by iUniverse.com, Inc.

For information address:
iUniverse.com, Inc.
620 North 48th Street, Suite 201
Lincoln, NE 68504-3467
www.iuniverse.com

Originally published by Dimension

ISBN: 0-595-00635-3

Printed in the United States of America

DEDICATION

I dedicate this book to my husband Ed, to my sons and their wives, Ed III and Cindy, Jim and Sandy, Tim and Sharon, and to my daughter Stephanie and her husband Mark. A special dedication goes to my three grandsons, Blake, Chad and Evan Wallace.   Patricia F. Wallace

I dedicate this book to my parents, Harvey and Emily Shepherd, and to my friend, Willie Ada Alix..   Sr. Mary Winifred, C.H.S.

Jointly, we dedicate this book to the memory of Frances whose spiritual journey was the inspiration for our writing.

ACKNOWLEDGEMENTS

There are many people we want to acknowledge and thank, beginning with Ed Wallace, the Reverend Mother Madeleine Mary, and the Sisters of the Community of the Holy Spirit, whose support made it possible for us to write this book.

We also want to thank the women who took the time to answer our questionnaire, and especially those twelve women whose stories appear in the book.

And we would like to thank our publisher Thomas Coffey, who was willing to make our work available to readers everywhere, for his encouragement, and for his probing questions.

The Twelve Steps are reprinted with permission of Alcoholics Anonymous World Services, Inc. Permission to reprint and adapt the Twelve Steps does not mean that A.A. has reviewed or approved the contents of this publication nor that A.A. agrees with the views expressed herein. A.A. is a program of recovery from alcoholism — use of the Twelve Steps in connection with programs and activities which are patterned after A.A., but which address other problems, does not imply otherwise.

Contents

Introduction

We have written this book for women. More particularly, this book is for recovering women who use the Twelve Steps as an essential part of their daily lives. We will focus on spirituality as defined by us and by these women. As one woman said, "My recovery *is* the story of my spirituality."

As authors, we are not negating the male experience of spirituality in recovery, nor are we saying that some of the feelings, qualities and actions presented here are not theirs also. What we are saying is that this book is for and about women.

How did this book come about? As friends talking together about various spiritual struggles, we remembered the difficulties one friend had with her spiritual search. She could never quite grasp it — the concept of spirituality. But just by seeking, she was already on a spiritual journey, only she did not know it. And so the book began. A book for those of us who sometimes feel that we don't "measure up" spiritually or even know what standard of measurement to use.

Some women may interpret spirituality as mystical experiences, an energy force, nature, etc. For us in writing this book, spirituality is the willingness to believe and trust in a Power greater than ourselves, encouraging us to grow in self-understanding with others. It also seeks to show through the stories and our own writing, that spirituality for most of us is found in the process of daily living, in the very ordinary and mundane, in the here and now. Seeing spirituality in this form keeps us in the absolute present. Whether we are able to acknowledge it or not, spirituality is an integral aspect of our being. It is part of the very fabric of living itself.

This book explains how spirituality enables us to grow in self-value, to govern and direct our feelings, and to build sound relationships with others. The intent of this book is to use the tools of Twelve Step programs to grow spiritually, hopefully enabling each of you to begin to "recreate" yourself. This re-creation is to be someone who is totally you — just you.

We believe that if you are using the Twelve Steps in your life then you are already on a spiritual journey. The questions that remain are: How do we take this journey? Who else will we find along the way? How far will we go? What will it be like? We want you to discover what we have discovered — self, willingness, hope, serenity, energy, relaxation, pleasure, encouragement, freedom and a sense of community.

As part of this endeavor, we have included with each chapter stories of women in recovery as well as questions for you to ask yourselves. You'll see that each of the women has a different spiritual understanding, but one that makes sense to her. The aim of these stories is to help us relate to one another.

the numerous women who participated in our survey. If you are interested in the survey, it is included in an appendix at the back of the book. There are many ways to get to the same place. This is our journey. This is your journey. Please come along!

The search for a spiritual path is as old as recorded history. It is our attempt to discover meaning in and for our lives, to relate to a Higher Power and to each other. Everyone is free to discover her own spirituality, her own path of spiritual growth; and yet there are persistently common, recurring themes woven throughout, whether we search intellectual depths or examine the events and relationships of everyday living. These themes include *self-value, adaptability of our feelings,* and *sound relationships.* Inherent in *self-value* are self-esteem, self-care, self-help and self-confidence. *Adaptability of feelings* allows us to be appropriate with our anger, joy, intolerance, patience and the whole range of emotional responses. *Sound relationships* imply a balanced give-and-take, trust, intimacy, openness and vulnerability.

Spirituality may be defined in traditional terms or may be interpreted as a mystical experience, an energy force, nature, cosmic space, etc. We have chosen to define spirituality as the willingness to believe and trust in a Power greater than ourselves, encouraging us to grow in self-understanding and in relationships with others. We contend that spirituality is found in the process of daily living.

Pause and consider:

- Addictions affect women in three areas: mental, physical and spiritual. Spiritual well-being is often the first quality lost in chemical dependency and the last regained in recovery. Has this been true in your life?
- How do you define spirituality so that it works for you?
- Can you think of an everyday task that you could look at in a new way so as to see the spirituality in your choice?

Spirituality and Women

One of the greatest challenges to us as women is to discover the spiritual qualities such as serenity, thoughtfulness, joy, gratitude, kindness to self and others, hidden within the routine of everyday life. We fill many roles: creator, nurturer, worker and lover. We need to see the spiritual qualities in what we do, who we are, and what we think and feel.

As creators, we are first and foremost birth-givers — not only human, physical birth, but birth-givers to ideas, relationships, art, music and drama.

We give birth to home and family life. We express our creative talents and abilities in making safe places and caring communities, not only in our homes, but also in our work places. With the creator position, though, comes the dichotomy of pain and joy. Nowhere is this more pronounced than in the pain of childbirth and in the joy of the co-creation of another human being. There is the pain of argument and misunderstanding balanced by the joy of reconciliation; tiredness and frustration, offset by a sense of accomplishment.

Too often we put ourselves last and believe this is the better way. We need to understand that by taking care of ourselves first, we are then able to take care of others. We tend to push the talents we possess into the recesses of our consciousness, always waiting for "just the right time." Too often, something else comes first. We stay awake long after the house is quiet to make time for these pursuits, rather than give them their rightful place. We discount our talents as frivolous and unnecessary. Sometimes it is difficult to know where to go with these gifts, and we need to stay quiet and listen for direction from our Higher Power. One artist said, "I am waiting for some direction from God as to where I am to go with my painting. Right now I am just waiting, secure that when the time is right, I will know what to do."

An outgrowth of our creativity is our capacity to nurture. In our culture, this is often considered a "woman's" word. It is defined by women. Nurturing includes feeding, encouraging, sustaining, supporting, naming — it is all of these, but more — it is giving and taking. Naming occupies an important place in our lives. How do you answer, "Who are you?" We do this with our names. Naming helps to define us. Think about the care given to choosing a child's name. It is an important task. We also name other things in our lives — our pets, those we treasure, the various rooms in our homes, our creations such as a book or poem, a painting, and a myriad of things that play a part in our lives. This may extend to what name we have for our Higher Power.

Give some thought to the following:

- Is it important for you to name your Higher Power?
- If the name is a non-traditional one, such as Goddess or Spirit Within, are you comfortable with the name you have chosen? For example, Sophia (Wisdom).
- If not, what would make it more comfortable?

- Are you uncomfortable with a feminine concept of a Higher Power?

We are caregivers. We parent our children (and sometimes our husbands and partners), we grandparent our children's children, and eventually we may even parent our parents. What a job! It seems never-ending and it can be, unless we pause and question whether or not we nurture ourselves as well as we take care of others. Nurturing can overwhelm us so that we reserve too little space of our own. "You have got to be kidding," commented one young mother, new to recovery, "I barely have enough time to take care of all that's necessary to do for the family. Making time for myself is a luxury I can't afford right now." How often do we say this to ourselves?

Prior to recovery, and sometimes well into sobriety, we neglect ourselves. How often do I take time to buckle my seat belt? Do I get a yearly mammography examination? When was my last visit to the dentist? Am I still smoking? Do I go to a therapist when I need additional help? One woman answered, "Sometimes, on my spiritual journey, I feel alone and need 'extra' help and counseling." It follows that to be a nurturer requires sufficient self-nurturing.

How do we define our role as worker? Society has trouble with this, so it's only natural that we do. There is an overlap between roles. Nowhere is this more pronounced than when we try to explain women as workers. There is tension about whether we work inside or outside the home. And what does this "inside or outside the home" represent? Some women receive financial compensation for work done within the house, although this same work could be done in an office setting — the clinician with a private practice in her home, the professional writer, the doctor with an office at home. On the other hand, there are women who are the community volunteers at hospitals, churches, homeless shelters and soup kitchens. Often unpaid work is not valued. This begins with us. Women must be the first to attach importance to what they do, rather than allowing others to define this for them. Ask the mother who is out of step with "work" today, who stays home with her children, or who must combine outside work with home duties. Is she proud of what she does? Does it make her feel good? "I have always chided my husband because it appears that he only pays lip service to the value of the work that I do to keep our home running smoothly," commented one woman in an interview, "then it dawned on me, I don't really place much importance on this type of work, so why should he?" Our work has value because of the importance we attach to it. Spirituality, when examined in these terms, helps us define ourselves.

Our role as lover is a complicated one, covering a broad basis of relationships: friend, mate, mother, companion, daughter. Webster's Dictionary defines lover as "one who loves," and "as a person who enjoys something deeply, as art." Included in our role as lover is our relationship with a Higher Power. Into all of these relationships, we can bring peace and harmony, or chaos and discord. It is as lover that we can instill confidence and trust. But it is also as lovers that we can manipulate and destroy. We've all seen the sweatshirt that jokingly says, "When Mom's happy, everybody's happy." There is a lot of truth in this statement, not only about mothers, but about women in general. We have the ability to be the emotional barometers in certain situations. This role, once given or taken, has the capacity to be very powerful.

Before recovery, at times in place of love, there was anger, jealousy, resentment, envy and hate.

With sobriety came the realization that there is no spirituality without love, love of self and love of others. Genuine love is incongruent with manipulation, possessiveness, abusiveness and control.

A part of our relationship with a Higher Power may be liturgical or religious observance, but it is more than this. It may include prayer and meditation. Though Twelve Step programs suggest that we return to our formal religious "connection" if we have one, this is not a necessity. Some maintain long-term recovery and significant spirituality without ever returning to a church affiliation. Take the time to decide what is right for you.

Spirituality touches us each in very unique ways. One grandmother said, "These are some of the joys I have known: a time of quiet on a porch in the spring, when the eyes drink in the green of the trees against the blue of the sky, the ears hear the song of a bird, the skin picks up the hint of a cooling breeze; a time of intimacy with close friends, of sharing experiences over a cup of tea; a time together with a grandchild, knowing you are trusted and loved."

Spiritual growth for some women may be blocked by the patriarchal, male-dominated stance often presented by theology and even by Alcoholics

Anonymous itself. Our newfound freedom and independence allow us, as women, to deviate from patriarchal spirituality to claim a more feminine approach as our own. This is not to disregard the traditional views, but to add to and expand upon them. It is risk taking, especially in early recovery, to present a different viewpoint, but the very essence of spirituality is meant to be free and permission-giving.

One member of a religious order said, "As I change, my relationship and understanding of God changes. I've gone from seeing God as patriarchal and Roman Catholic, to an idea, to spirit, to one with the universe, to a holistic life force, to a feminine presence." Spirituality is ever-evolving.

The Twelve Steps, Recovery and Spirituality

Twelve Step programs are recognized as one of the most successful means of recovery, but the idea of spirituality as a component of recovery pre-dates A.A. Carl Jung, noted psychoanalyst, was one of the first to appreciate that spirituality and recovery depend on each other. The Twelve Steps provide a framework for spiritual growth, a framework that can benefit those of us who have been described as suffering the consequences of "self-will run riot."

What can these Twelve Steps do to aid us in containing this self-will of ours? They can help us begin a new way of thinking, possibly a new way of exploring our individual concept of spirituality. As you read this book you may see your Higher Power in a different light, a light that frees you to validate your own beliefs.

Step One Story

A professional woman, tells of her struggle in recovery...

My drinking career did not begin until I was twenty-eight. After the birth of my second child, I was suffering from acute depression, and my doctor suggested that I have a few beers each day to help me relax. Every day for the next ten years, I drank. My chief concern was planning when and how I would drink each day. In the last year of my drinking I began to promise myself that I wouldn't drink, but I did anyway. I returned to college and I still drank. I began working full time so that I would not be home so much and I still found time to drink. I tried everything I knew to control my drinking and nothing was successful. Finally I decided to try a self-help group. But the daily compulsion to drink continued, and I believed that I was going insane, that I had done irreversible brain damage. However, I did learn to put off the first drink one minute at a time. I was told to keep coming back, and I did. I did not believe in a Higher Power, but I was encouraged to be as honest, open-minded and willing as I could be, and I followed those directions.

Slowly, I began to see that some things were changing in my life, things that couldn't be "coincidences." I began to wonder, "Maybe there is a Higher Power." This was my first conscious awareness of my spiritual journey.

I clung to the people in A.A. I was afraid to be away from them. I did not know how to live without something to dull the pain and fear. I did not trust my own judgments. The group supported me and assured me that what I was experiencing was normal and that it would pass. And it did. The group became a Higher Power for me. I could not stay sober on my own, but when I came to meetings I was able not to pick up a drink. I also found my sense of isolation and loneliness disappeared at meetings. Gradually everything began to make sense to me: I understood that when I drank I could not guarantee what I would say or do. I was powerless in this area of my life. Alcohol was the boss — a power greater than I was.

It has been sixteen years since I first entered the rooms of Alcoholics Anonymous. I did not come to A.A. because I wanted to stop drinking. I did not believe I was an alcoholic. I came to learn how to drink like normal people.

The first step says, "We admitted we were powerless..." but I could not accept that I was powerless over anything or anybody. "God, if there is a God, help me to be willing to be willing." This was my first attempt at prayer. I repeated it frequently. My experience was not the blinding light variety — it was a long and difficult path.

These revelations of alcohol and the group as having power greater than I were the first steps on an inner journey. The keys of willingness, honesty and openmindedness unlocked inner doors. By admitting powerlessness over alcohol, I became empowered to become all that I could become.

I used to think of spirituality as religion. Now, it has a much deeper meaning. Coming to know who I am, what I am capable of, the power of honesty and how it nurtures my evolving self are a part of spirituality. Being able to live in harmony with self and others is a bit more. Love of the me who has been born in recovery is another facet of this journey. My spiritual journey has come to be the knowledge of who, what and why I am. It is knowledge gained through powers greater than myself and a personal belief in a Power that answered an honest prayer, "God, if there is a God, help me to be willing to be willing."

Step One

We admitted we were powerless over alcohol and that our lives had become unmanageable.

"The most important step I took was to admit I was powerless over my addiction — that my life had become unmanageable." This statement from one woman's story is typical of the practicality and simplicity needed to begin and continue in a Twelve Step program.

Recognizing and admitting powerlessness over a particular substance or activity is not fun or easy, and for most comes at the end of much suffering, exhaustion and pain. But here, you are finally able to acknowledge that you cannot manage your own life. For many, perhaps for all, the time just before taking this First Step is one of feeling personally worthless, emotionally out of control, alone and friendless.

Women new to recovery most often are coming out of an isolated existence, if they are not physically separated, then they are at least emotionally apart. Usually the combination of both exists. You commonly hear the following when you listen to what women say at meetings: "I don't have any friends. I'm afraid of other women. I just don't trust anyone. I have always felt out of place, even in my own home." Because of these feelings and because of the familiarity of the isolation, becoming an active participant in a recovery program can be a very scary place to find yourself. You might not like the aloneness you feel, but you certainly are accustomed to it. If at this point in time you are new to recovery and possibly even newer to acknowledging your budding spirituality, you will want to consider creating for yourself a safe place — a haven where you can feel protected and secure. A place to experiment with your newfound thoughts and feelings.

Weigh how you feel about the following:

- When you think back, have you often felt "different"?
- Do you have women friends? If not, why not?
- Are you able to trust other women?
- List some qualities you would like in a new woman friend.
- Do you possess any of these qualities you are looking for?

Without a proper grounding in Step One, recovery cannot be long-lasting. First, there is the awareness that indeed something is very wrong in your life, and then you begin to lay the foundation for a healthy renewal of your life. This foundation can begin with a safe space. In the beginning when everything is new and unfamiliar, this safe place may only be available to you within your inner being. Soon the meetings themselves will become a refuge. One woman with well over forty years in A.A. put it this way: "When you are new in this program, try not to bring the same stress into the rooms of A.A. as you must deal with in your everyday life. Use the program as a haven, as a place to 'let your hair down' and be yourself. After all you have your whole life to work these steps." Later as you develop a deeper understanding of your program you will begin to enlarge your safe space. This place will foster your recovery and enhance your spirituality. How will this happen? By including in this area the people, places and things that nurture you on your journey. As we have said in our introduction, we want you to discover what we have discovered and being capable of creating a safe space is part of that discovery.

Reflect upon the following:
- Do you have a safe place?
- Can you think of how to create your particular space?

- Can you envision including one other trustworthy woman in your place? Who would that be?

As you begin to integrate these concepts into your life you will begin to pave a way to grow in *self-value, adaptability of feelings* and *sound relationships.* This growth promotes a wholeness of self which enables you to develop strength and energy.

Beginning a Twelve Step program provides a sense of belonging that will enable you to find your truest identity. This may seem like a paradox — a mystery — but by joining together with others who can most fully understand you, you are able to become yourself. A relative newcomer to a Twelve Step program said, "I was never an individual until I surrendered and began building a new me. Everyone was an authority figure to me; I did not know how to stand on my own two feet. I followed this program for ten years before I truly accepted my disease and surrendered. I tried to do it my way — it was a painful, lonely existence."

The emphasis on *we* and belonging will make the recognition of your powerlessness empowering rather than self-defeating. If powerlessness were a tangible symptom of a physical illness, like the pain one feels when a stomach ulcer has developed, you certainly would consider it foolish to ignore it. Not so with the clues that present themselves as signs of mental and/or emotional illnesses. Why is there such willingness to endure the pain associated with those less visible diseases and disorders? Are you still victimized by the stigma of alcoholism, eating disorders, emotions out of control, or depression? If so, becoming willing to admit to powerlessness over the present situation and joining a support group is the first step phase of placing *value* on yourself. A woman wrote, "I looked at my self-esteem through others' appraisal of me, my abilities and my assets. I was even dominated by the A's I received in graduate school. Anything less than an A equaled failure." In the beginning, the acknowledgment of support group members is needed to bolster sagging self-esteem. At this stage, dependence on other-esteem, something outside yourself, may be a necessary ingredient to make you feel valuable. This is just as it should be in early recovery. It is important to distinguish the helpful regard of others from the unhealthy dependence experienced prior to using the Twelve Steps in your life.

Contemplate:
- Do you see the constructive aspects of admitting to being powerless? If so, what are they?
- Do the members of your group help you to see the value you have as a human being and as a woman?
- Are you beginning to see some of your good qualities?

Does anyone not know the feelings of guilt, anger, resentment and despair? With any addiction these feelings are magnified, but by taking Step One — admitting that you are powerless over your addiction and that your life is unmanageable — you begin to be able to adapt your feelings and adjust your responses.

One young member of N.A. wrote, "I was unable to express my anger before coming to the program. It was an emotion I had to learn to feel. I feared anger in every aspect. As I become more in touch with my anger and less afraid of it, I am less troubled by it and more able to find constructive, healthy outlets and channels for it." Another woman said, "I was never even aware that I was jealous until I was sober for a while. Now I acknowledge feelings of jealousy when they come up and try to work through them by talking and praying."

Step One invites you to get to know your feelings. Here you begin to give a name to those vague emotions that seem to control you.

How would you answer the following:
- What feelings can you name today?
- What feelings do you think control you today?
- What feelings give you the most trouble?

As you work on your addiction issues and things appear to be falling into place for you, be aware that this is the time when other dependencies may begin to arise. You will not be the first to realize that you may be staying late at the office day after day, drinking too much caffeine, neglecting family responsibilities to attend more meetings than you really need, eating enormous amounts of sugar, etc. This substitution happens and you need to pause every now and then and check yourself out in these other areas. This is part and parcel of nurturing yourself. Remember also that at this stage of recovery you are very fragile so be gentle with yourself if you recognize that you have changed dependencies. Since you are probably new to this concept of *self-value*, you may need to learn by modeling. You do this by watching and imitating someone whose style you like. Look around the meeting rooms, your office, or home and see who takes care of herself in a healthy way. Do what she does, and if you can't figure out how she does it — ask her. That's right, just take a deep breath and do it. You might be surprised at how simple it really is.

Surely no one enters a recovery program without having fractured relationships. At this early stage, you can only scratch the surface of the work you will want to do to improve the relationships in your life. In the beginning, this task looks almost impossible. Patience is needed: all improvement takes time. "I have been able to form a relationship with myself for the first time, then with my husband. Neither could have happened without the help of God and A.A.," one woman said. And another woman wrote, "Forming relationships is a process. I am learning to give of myself, but not to give myself away totally."

Consider for a moment:
- What is a healthy relationship for you?
- What healthy relationships did you have before entering your Twelve Step program?
- What healthy relationships do you have today?

You must give yourself the time and space to let *healthy relationships* develop. For some, sobriety brings the first opportunity to establish and develop relationships based on openness and trust. A chance to try your hand at a healthy friendship may first begin with your sponsor in the program. A sponsor is a woman who will help you understand what recovery, using a Twelve Step program, is about. She will show you this by sharing with you her "experience, strength and hope." As we go along in this book, we will talk more about a sponsor's role in your life. You will discover more new friends, but you will also have much mending to do in relationships with old friends and family. And you may even have to face the fact that some prior relationships are damaged beyond repair. In the coming steps of your program you will find the tools and approaches for mending and maintaining *sound relationships.*

Looking ahead, Step One can continue to work for you. As recovery progresses, the powerlessness and unmanageability that this step addresses will become evident in other areas of your life. One woman with long-term sobriety said, "I continue to be amazed at how much is really out of my control. I can't live my child's life for him; I can't save him from the mistakes he needs to make. I would love to be able to, but that is not the way life is designed. A.A. has given me the ability to step back and look at a situation and see whether or not it is something that would be healthy for me to control. If it is not my problem, I can leave it and get on with my day."

Before going on, consider:

- Where do unmanageability and powerlessness fit into everyday situations for you?
- What place does Step One have in your life today? Can you see this place changing?

Step One is your connection to a new way of living — a new life, free from addiction, open to new choices, full of possibilities for creativity and freedom, and maybe most important, the discovery of you — in all your wonder and uniqueness.

Step Two Story

Relapse is part of this woman's story...

My story can easily be summed up by the saying I've heard around A.A. rooms for a long time: "I drank too much for too long!" In my case, that "too long" was twenty-four years.

Drinking contributed to my flunking out of a prestigious women's college, four years of a rocky and physically abusive marriage, lost jobs, low-paying positions and squandered savings. Alcohol and drugs frequently made me feel like the person I wasn't, but wanted to be. These substances were never really my friends, but they were definite mood and perception changes. Sometimes I just drank because I had nothing else to do; other times because I had so much to do.

In A.A., insanity is often described as doing the same thing and expecting different results. That's just what I did. There were good times, I suppose, but most of my memories of those years are filled with hurt, shame, disgust, turmoil and immoral behavior.

My first Higher Power in A.A. was what the literature suggests it might be — the A.A. group. I attended a commuters' group which met five days a week starting at 5:30 p.m. Those meetings and the people who attended helped keep me sober for three years. In my drinking days, I would have been in a bar after work at 5:30 p.m., but the commuters' groups gave me a new pattern to follow. But the literature of A.A. warns that there will come a time when you have no defense against that first drink except by turning to your Higher Power and sometimes that can't be a group. I learned the truth of this when I relapsed because I could not or would not reach out to my personal Higher Power.

My Higher Power is a God of my understanding. Many times that God is Good Orderly Direction, *and very often through meetings, phone calls or other contacts, that God is a* Group of Drunks.

Since January 1988, I have lived an evolving, much more serene life in A.A. and that is due to my developing belief in a God that I understand and can truly relate to.

Step Two

Came to believe that a power greater than ourselves could restore us to sanity.

Step Two is evidence of hope. With Step One you may have hit bottom when you admitted and acknowledged the powerlessness and the unmanageability in your life, but Step Two is an open window, a signal and sign that there is a way out of misery and apparent failure. There *is* a greater power — a power greater than your addiction. Step Two, like Step One, is reflective in character: it asks you to allow your beliefs and hopes, however weak or small they may seem, to take root and begin to grow. You do not have to name the higher power in your life or get in touch with it, but only believe that such a power exists. Sometimes the only recognition that there is a higher power may come through other group members: you can see that their lives have been turned around, and so you will risk trusting that your life can be changed too.

Step Two is freeing and empowering. Although some women may quickly improve their existing relationship with a familiar Higher Power, you do

not have to associate your beliefs with any organized religion. "I am beginning to relate to my spirituality as a source from within," one new member
of A.A. said, "rather than that which is bestowed on
me from the altar or by traditional examples of
'spiritual things'." Until recently, male theologians
have dictated to women what their spirituality
should be. Women are now beginning to determine
this for themselves and the feminine is being intro-
duced into the realm of the sacred in ways creatively
appropriate to our cultural times and experiences.

For other women, the path toward belief is a
very slow and arduous one. "I wanted to believe in a
Higher Power," one woman wrote, "but for a long
time I struggled thinking that I had to have answers
to all my complex intellectual questions."

If you are using the Twelve Steps in your life,
then you are already on a spiritual journey. Again,
simply stated, spirituality is the willingness to believe and trust in a Power greater than ourselves,
encouraging us to grow in *self-value, adaptability of
feelings* and *sound relationships*. How do you set
out on this path towards growth? It may be that you
will begin with a different view of the spiritual —
that which you hold sacred. One concept you could
use is that the very fact of life is testimony to the

spiritual. This says that spirituality exists from within rather than coming down from on high or from outside ourselves. Spirituality *is*, rather than spirituality *will be*. This may take some thinking about if you have grown up believing that spirituality is something that we learn — something taught — rather than a presence that needs cultivating.

Would it be easier for you if:

- Spirituality had a more feminine side?
- You could believe that you are already a spiritual woman?

Step Two's second part, "restore us to sanity," is troublesome to most newcomers to A.A. Many come to A.A. with the hope that if they stop drinking they will not go insane. Reading Step Two infers that you were insane and a restoration has begun. It is possible to look at this as the insanity of the disease. While some who are in recovery truly experienced insanity in its fullest meaning, most understand this step to mean the insanity of your disease. Can you see the insanity of living life each day believing that addiction will provide permanent relief from anxiety, make fantasy into reality, and make all your dreams come true? Looking back on the days before recovery began, you will be able to see just how insane your behavior, feelings and actions really were. "I was sure I was going crazy," one woman said. "There was a dialog inside my head that explained how good I would feel if I'd just have *one* drink — and I listened to those voices for years, but I had never stopped with one drink. Step Two made me realize that I didn't have to drink in response to that dialog. I began to believe that I could react differently."

Pause again and reflect on these questions:
- Have any of your actions at least bordered on "insanity"? When? How?
- Is there an inner dialog that rationalizes your compulsive behavior when you feel uncomfortable or unsure of yourself?

Step Two is an assurance that feelings of unworthiness, fear, guilt and remorse can be dealt with and converted into positive feelings of self-worth, forgiveness and confidence. We have chosen to write about Step Two not as a question of whether sanity can or will be restored, but as a positive statement. We, the authors, and a large majority of the women who answered our questionnaire, believe that a Higher Power has restored us from addiction to a greater sanity, and that is the message that we want to share. Growth in both recovery and spirituality, indicates sanity. Healthy recovery sustains itself in reality; in the same way, healthy spirituality is grounded in the present, produces joy and a lively sense of humor, an appreciation for beauty, and a balanced concern for others. One woman wrote, "I now have a consistent feeling of faith, that whatever unfolds for me in life is meant to be and will somehow give me beneficial growth. I feel capable of being a healing channel."

"Restored to sanity" doesn't mean that everything in life will be clear and easy, but that you will have a way of coping with the painful and difficult aspects of life. Believing and trusting that a Higher Power can restore you to sanity allows you to be more circumspect and objective, to form priorities, and to adapt your feelings and emotional responses. "I used to get very upset over interruptions in my work schedule," one woman recalled, "but I'm learning to ask myself 'how important is it?' — usually the interruptions are not significant enough for the emotional energy that I've given them in the past."

"Life is something like a hurricane," a young member of N.A. said. "On the outer edges there are turmoil, destruction, chaos, fear and violence. You are tossed about, a helpless victim of winds and waves over which you have no control. But if you quit fighting the storm, you can move into the peace of the center where there is calm, trust, faith, hope, love, joy and most of all, a belief that somehow all things will be okay — not the absence of trouble, but the realization of the presence of a Power higher than yourself."

A much older member of A.A. expressed her experience, strength and hope this way: "I, who over eighteen years ago fell off a chair and crawled to the sofa, recently conducted a large corporate meeting. Sure, I like myself, am proud to be where I am...but I didn't do it by myself — God and the fellowship of A.A. helped."

There are simple, everyday instances of joy too, times when you *know* you are sane and well. You not only begin to feel an emotional balance, but also a sense of awe and wonder, and personal relationships become stronger and healthier as well. One sign of sanity is the ability to find and appreciate the good and beautiful. Addiction, and its preoccupation with compulsive behavior, dulled recognition and sensitivity. Now sober, you have an opportunity to re-discover, or perhaps discover for the first time, the wonders of every day: the feel of the wind on your face; the sounds of bumblebees, laughing children, barking dogs; the smell of a favorite food or newly mown grass; the colors at sunrise or sunset; the graceful lines and patterns in architecture or decorative stenciling. Another outgrowth of sobriety — of sanity — is your ability to share discoveries and feelings with others. Let the hope and joy of Step Two form and foster friendships and sound relationships.

Pause and consider:

- What "everyday" instances of joy can you name for yourself?
- Do you take time — even a few minutes — to enjoy the beauty around you?
- What "discovery" can you share with another woman today?
- How do *you* feel about living today?

"Sobriety via the Steps has enabled me to move through fear and to face myself and the world. I am *excited* about living today, pursuing dreams and creativity. Down moments are just that — temporary," said one A.A. member. And another woman, not yet far into recovery, responded, "Yes, I know that my Higher Power has restored me to sanity — when I arrange a bouquet of flowers, hang the laundry outdoors just for a 'windblown' smell, listen to the contented purr of my cat — I realize how many treasures I had refused and neglected in favor of my compulsive behavior."

Once again, Step Two gives evidence of hope. It is a preparation for a deepening belief in your ability to recover. Step Two is a building block in the basics that will enable your sobriety and deepening spirituality.

Step Three Story

An artist working to build upon her existing spiritual concept writes...

I am in a Twelve Step program because I need to be.

I don't remember much about my childhood, but I do remember that my parents drank and when they drank, they drank too much. I can see today that because of their drinking their behavior was unusual in comparison to that of other parents: they were unhappy; they didn't look forward to life.

Growing up I never felt "quite right." I always craved attention, and got it by pretending to be sick. I drank once or twice in high school, but I didn't know that drugs existed until I went to college. There I smoked pot and that led to the more serious drugs. Drug use destroyed my first marriage. Our marriage didn't have a chance. He was an alcoholic and a drug addict — he was my supplier. I prayed, and I received the courage to stop drugs and to leave him, then I started to drink.

I remarried, still drinking, still craving attention, still pretending to be sick. I got pregnant for *the first time, and stopped drinking. I had the baby, and started drinking again. Drinking was still in the controlled stage. But by the time I got pregnant with my second child, I couldn't control my drinking. Alcoholism just took me. I prayed every night not to drink, but I was not able to stop. I had to drink. I knew I was an alcoholic but I could not imagine not drinking. I ended up in detox.*

When I was there, I completely surrendered. That is where the gift started. I had no idea of the journey I was going to be on — the growing I would have to do. It was all because of my faith that I was able to begin my journey, and that I am still able to continue today.

A.A. has given me spirituality which is probably what I had before but could not define. The steps in A.A. outline how to live a spiritual life. Even now, when I study the Bible, it just confirms what A.A. teaches in its steps. There is feeling in the rooms of A.A., a feeling of fellowship and closeness that is indescribable. In an A.A. meeting it feels safe; we all belong there. I always learn by hearing how someone else handles a situation. That enables me to leave the rooms of A.A. armed with new information to implement in my daily living.

A.A. meetings are free and open. We are free to express our spirituality as we experience it, in contrast to organized religion which expects us to conform to a specific viewpoint.

At this time in my life I just can't go to church. A.A. has taken priority in my spiritual life. I see religion as believing in rules and regulations, while spirituality is about me and my feelings and my relationship with God. I believe that spirituality is part of life, not something divorced from it. I think the amount of fulfillment you get from this program depends on how important the steps are and how willing you are to follow them. There is a peace and serenity about those people who practice the steps.

I was very willing to take Step Three. This step means living life on life's terms and accepting what comes. It is about trusting God. The Serenity Prayer was and is a big part of my sobriety. This is where I began to put my program into action. Spirituality has everything to do with serenity. Spirituality gives me peace of mind. It is the turning over of my life and will to the care of God. For example, God gave me the gift of being able to paint, but I'm not sure how to use it right now. I am turning it over to God just to hold onto it for me. I am willing, but I am just waiting for the answer to be made clear to me. I be-

lieve as each day unfolds, the answers for that day
come with it. I thank God every day for the trust,
love and faith I have in Him.

Step Three

Made a decision to turn our will and our lives over to the care
of God *as we understood Him.*

As you have seen before, Step One and Step
Two are largely reflective in nature and content. In
Step One you considered how powerless and unmanageable your life had become, and in Step Two
you came to believe that only a Power greater than
yourself could restore order and sanity to your life.

But now, it is time to come face to face with
Step Three, and the space for reflection has become
a time for action. The decision to turn your will and
your life over to the care of a Higher Power — to
God as you understand God — is as crucial a step in
your developing spirituality as it is in your recovery,
and in your continuing sobriety. God as you understand God leaves you free to choose whatever image
of a Higher Power works for you. In *As Bill Sees It,*
A.A.'s co-founder states:

> We are only operating a spiritual kinder-
> garten in which people are enabled to get
> over drinking and find the grace to go on
> living to better effect. Each man's
> [woman's] theology has to be his [her] own
> quest, his [her] own affair. (p. 95)

As discussed in Chapter One, you need not be
bound by the conservative or the traditional, nor are
you to be impeded by the male-oriented language of
A.A. "My present religious preference is not an organized religion; rather I believe in a Universal
Energy, and the Goddess Spirit within," said one
woman in A.A. Choose what is comfortable and
what works for you, and then strive to become more
and more at ease with your choice.

Have you given any thought to:
- What part does your fear of making mistakes
  play in your spiritual concept?
- Does the concept you have of a Higher Power
  allow for your healthy development as a
  woman?

At first it may be necessary or may put you
more at ease if you think of your recovery group as
a higher power. This collective energy — a group of
women working together on a common problem —

can and does work for a lot of people. We need only to look at this collective power in the Women's Movement and the effect it has had throughout the world. What could not be done individually, women banding together have accomplished. For some, this group concept is one they choose to stay with. For others this is a beginning and their concept changes. There is not right or wrong here. Take possession of what is yours.

Suppose your Higher Power concept breaks with tradition and takes on a feminine identity or Nature, or a Presence Within? You will be taking a risk by stepping out of the mainstream, but as women begin to use their legitimate power, these ideas and beliefs will become more and more acceptable. We will discuss legitimate power further on in this book. A look at history and literature shows that Goddess as deity is certainly not a new idea. A visit to Greece, Italy or France shows artistic proof of the value of the feminine in a Higher Power. Goddesses in the form of statues, paintings, frescoes, etc. abound in these cultural centers of Europe. The deity perspective of Nature is seen in the Native American concept of spirituality. In the Hindu tradition, the gods are closely related to the forces of nature with the universe being divided into three sections: the earth, the atmosphere and the heavens. This division provides the framework for classifying the gods. These are but a handful of the possibilities open to you to incorporate into your spiritual life. Take the time to decide what concept can help you to develop a positive inner vitality, a vitality that will assist you in attaining *self-value, adaptability of feelings* and *sound relationships.*

There are two important aspects of Step Three that we must be careful not to minimize or discount. The first part, "made a decision," implies an act of commitment involving willingness and healthy dependence. In the literature of Alcoholics Anonymous, willingness has been called the "key" for unlocking the way to faith. For many, belief in a Higher Power cannot be understood intellectually. Understanding takes what many writers have called a "leap of faith," because there is no explanation that will satisfy your intellectual curiosity. Fortunately you are not asked or expected to have a detailed and rational explanation for your belief. Step Three requires only that you have a willingness to make a decision, to let go of your will and your life, into the trust and care of a Higher Power. The existence of willingness is evidence that spirituality is already at work in your life.

How can women, who are often too dependent on others to begin with, look on this suggestion of depending on a Higher Power in a constructive way? It helps to take a look at part of the explanation of Step Three given in A.A.'s *Twelve Steps and Twelve Traditions*. It is there we find:

> Every man and woman who has joined A.A. and intends to stick has, without realizing it, made a beginning on Step Three. Isn't it true that, in all matters touching upon alcohol, each of them has decided to turn his or her life over to the care, protection and guidance of A.A.?
>
> Already a willingness has been achieved to cast out one's own will and one's own ideas about the alcohol problem in favor of those suggested by A.A. Now if this is not turning one's will over to a newfound "Providence" then what is it? (pp. 36-37)

This suggests a removal of your dependence on various substances, food, attitudes, sex, etc., and an attachment to that which leads to a better quality of life — a new way of approaching the everyday. As you progress in your working of the Twelve Steps, you will be able to define more clearly for yourself the things that improve the essence of life. This new definition will lead to a better understanding of yourself, a firm grasp on how you react, and a healthy involvement with others.

In making a decision to turn your will and your life over to the care of a Higher Power, you exercise your spirituality and your spiritual gifts, and give yourself an opportunity to grow and become more fully yourself. It is here that you make a conscious effort to develop a pattern of self-care. For instance, you may begin to recognize your creative talents: talents to be used by you to fulfill your destiny. What about art as spiritual? The woman in the story for this step is an artist. This talent, newly discovered and constantly growing, has not been totally validated by her, nor has she absorbed to the fullest its importance to her as a whole person. Yet one only has to look at her work and listen when she talks about how it makes her feel, to see how truly spiritual this accomplishment is for her — how much it increases her *self-value*. Using your gifts will result in the healthy pride that is so necessary in the development of self-esteem and self-confidence.

Think about:
- Do you believe that you have certain creative talents? What are they?

- Can you see what you do in the everyday as an expression of your creativity? For example, preparing a meal, contributing to a project at the office, weeding the garden, or listening with attention to a friend.
- Are you developing your creativity so it enhances your quality of life?

A second vitally important aspect of Step Three is that you turn to God *as you understand Him.* You do not now — or ever — have to be able to define God or your Higher Power. Spirituality is not static or stagnant. Spirituality is ever-evolving in that your concept and understanding of your Higher Power, of your God, changes as you grow.

Most women find that a lot of willingness is required in taking Step Three, and that the effectiveness of their whole program depends on how persistently and well they work on this step. Some discover an inner well of willingness, based on an already firm faith in a Higher Power they can name and know. Others may struggle for years in an attempt to grasp at a concept of a Higher Power that seems just outside or beyond their reach.

"I was willing to take Step Three," one woman wrote, "but depending on what I want to control, it may be necessary to be willing all over again on a daily basis." Another woman wrote, "It depends on what day it is! Sometimes I need a little willingness to take Step Three and sometimes I need a lot. In stressful periods of my life, I need to take Step Three daily!"

Step Three is an essential aspect of your spiritual growth. Although it may seem paradoxical at first — that this is the opposite of the truth — you do, in fact, grow in *self-value* and self-worth by making the decision to turn your out-of-control life over to a Higher Power. Although this action may appear to be based on negative qualities such as "surrender" or even "failure," turning your will and your life over to Higher Power is actually an act of wisdom and strength. One woman wrote, "I find that as I become more open to God's will, I find more peace in my life."

Most would not consider it an act of surrender or failure if you called a carpenter to repair a leaky roof on your house, or if you had to hire a plumber to replace a broken pipe. Nor do you hesitate to consult an automobile mechanic about your too noisy car, an accountant about your income tax return, a pediatrician when your children are ill, or a dentist when you have a toothache. You regularly turn over the responsibility for your care to doctors, teachers, airplane pilots and taxi drivers. You are not unfamiliar with the concept of turning to others for help and assistance in your everyday life. Step Three emphasizes that the spiritual side of your life is a part of the whole, and points you in the direction of positive help in attaining sobriety and establishing *self-value*.

Step Three begins a life-long practice of pausing, stepping back from situations, discerning their importance, and asking for help and guidance to know the difference between your will and that which this Presence in your life has in mind for you. It then becomes easy to make the choice; that choice which will certainly result in healthy feelings about yourself, secure knowledge that your *feelings* are appropriate for the situation, and that your relationships are as they should be.

Just think about:
- Are you hesitant to work on Step Three? Why?
- Do fear, insecurity or arrogance hinder your ability to implement Step Three in your life?

Daily living presents you with far more problems than alcoholism, eating disorders, codependency and the like. Remorse and guilt; bitterness, anger, envy, jealousy and resentment, financial and material insecurity: all of these may threaten to overwhelm you with panic and despair. Turning to a Higher Power, acknowledging that you are not in control, frees you to accept and modify your *feelings.* "Spirituality is the turning over of my life and will to the care of God," one woman said. "I believe as each day unfolds, the answers for that day come with it." This turning over does not take away our responsibilities in life. It merely clarifies that which is ours to work on. It helps us to see when we are doing more than our share, when we are enabling others to escape their own duties, and it allows us to recognize and be comfortable with our accomplishments.

As an outgrowth of your developing self-value and your ability to accept and modify your feelings, you will discover a deeper soundness and wholesomeness in your personal *relationships.* Remember how detached you were from everyone and everything when you were in your old behaviors? Now you are able to become involved with others. Step Three is a powerful reminder that there is a danger in trying to be entirely self-sufficient — you do need a Higher Power, and in turning over your self-will and egotism, you allow this Presence, this Energy to come to you possibly through other human beings, maybe in traditional religion, and most certainly in your own creative process.

Ask yourself these questions:

- Has your relationship with your Higher Power improved since you began working on Step Three?
- Are you beginning to see how the unhealthy aspects of power and control diminished your essence of life?
- Are you beginning to have a better give-and-take relationship with the significant people in your life?

No discussion of Step Three would be complete without reference to the Serenity Prayer:

God grant me the serenity to accept the things I cannot change, courage to change the things I can, and wisdom to know the difference.

The dictionary defines serenity as the quality or state of being calm and quiet, free of storms or unpleasant change. Step Three invites you into serenity — into wisdom, courage and acceptance. "Part of serenity for me means that I have learned not to waste valuable time on negative thoughts. I know these emotions are okay, but to allow them to continue takes time away from thoughts and actions that are positive for me," wrote a woman in both A.A. and Al-Anon. You need to see serenity as a vital part of nurturing yourself. True serenity — that emotional and mental state of well-being — results in an inner and outer sense of evenness and peace.

Have you ever defined the following words with meanings that suit you and your life style? Try defining these words with meanings that suit you:

- *Serenity*
- *Joy*
- *Acceptance*
- *Healing*
- *Involvement*

Having worked the first three steps, you are now prepared with an adequate foundation to do the work necessary for Step Four.

Step Four Story

A member of a Catholic religious community explains her Fourth Step process...

I have been a member of a religious community for sixteen years. I learned to cope and hide so well that the community didn't know anything about my parents' alcoholism, or about my sexual abuse — everything looked good. We had Sisters trained in addictions counseling and intervention. I could have gotten help earlier, but no one knew that I needed it. I think what finally got me to go to a Twelve Step program was that I lost control — I couldn't cope. I didn't want to live. I remember feeling that something was drastically wrong, but I didn't want anybody to know. Every time I turned around I lost control. I thought once I hit thirty, it would all smooth out, but it was a mess.

I taught ethics and morality and yet I didn't believe a word of it. I taught that we are all bonded and interdependent, and I'd walk out and say, "I don't want to be in a relationship," because I hated me. I felt that I had no worth and no value other than what I could do. I didn't have any problem *applying God or spirituality or self-respect to others, but that didn't apply to me. I didn't really believe in anything that I said.*

I went from being one of the leaders in the community to being someone you couldn't find, absolutely isolated. I'm a professional artist, as well as a teacher, and in my community I found acceptance and motivation and challenge to be that creative person. When the community began to move in a healthier direction, allowing for therapy, attendance at self-help groups and rest time, I had no idea what they were saying. I saw myself as what I do, not who I am.

In my childhood my mother often locked me somewhere, maybe in the attic, maybe in the closet; my father sexually abused me when he was drunk. I believed all of this was my fault. Somehow I had caused it to happen.

Now I can say it was not my fault. One of the things that was so important when I first started attending Adult Children of Alcoholics meetings and the incest survivors' group, was to hear others say that I was not to blame. The total responsibility is on my parents' shoulders.

When I was thirty and my mother was diagnosed with cancer, my father called me. I ran home and took care of things. I was doing that because that was my identity, but it was tearing me apart. During one trip home, my dad tried to seduce me — I was thirty years old and this was still happening. I had been in therapy for six years, and the therapist had asked me if anything had happened. I told him that when I was nine I was raped by a neighbor, but I never told him that my dad set it up. I didn't tell him that my dad had abused me emotionally and used me as a substitute wife. I don't think I was ever treated as a child.

Combining A.C.O.A. meetings with therapy set me on a healthier path. Steps One, Two and Three were a beginning, but Step Four was the turning point. I did a relationship inventory first. I could see that I had to make a change or my life would get worse. At the time I had what I considered one emotionally healthy relationship — all the others had collapsed. I was very conscious of needing help.

For me, the Fourth Step isn't done once, but several times — each time it sinks in at another level. Having to write it was my biggest fear, because once it was written I couldn't deny it. One of the most helpful aspects of that step was that it was tangible — the first time I did it the thing that struck me was thorough *because I wanted to skip things and all that did was succeed in hiding them from me. I had to go back and try to be honest with myself, from my heart, rather than letting my head say "we can skip that part" — and that was very hard to do. I asked somebody to stay near me while I did the Fourth Step because I was scared to death. I thought, "I'm not going to be able to do this." For months I kept coming to Step Four and saying, "I can't do this." Finally I called another Sister and asked if she would come over. I just needed somebody to be in the house. When I finished I did not feel worthless. It was a very positive experience.*

In my community, in my job, and in my art, my sense of a Higher Power, of God, is global. When I go to meetings I can take that concept and apply it to myself — more a sense of the spirit within. Alcoholics Anonymous is an excellent example of a base community. Usually we don't know or acknowledge that living in community takes a lot of effort. The more authentic you are, the more centered, the more you are in touch with the sacred. Twelve Step groups are very freeing, they allow individuals to say "where I am right now is okay." I used to believe that human was not good enough — now I believe that human is just fine.

Step Four

Made a searching and fearless moral inventory of ourselves.

A natural outgrowth of Step Three — of making a decision to turn your will and your life over to the care of God *as you understand Him* — is your beginning readiness to take Step Four: to make a fearless moral inventory. While it is not necessary to take the Twelve Steps in order, you may find it easier to do so particularly at this point, because of the way one step builds on the next. Step Three provides a transition from willingness and healthy dependence into the courage and self-confidence of Step Four.

The spiritual growth that begins even tentatively in the first three steps is able to develop and expand in Step Four. You can only continue to grow spiritually — in *self-value,* in *adaptability of feelings,* and in *sound relationships with others* — when you make an inventory or take stock of exactly what strengths and weaknesses you have to work with. At this time in your recovery process, you may come to a realization of the extent of isolation and loneliness you experienced in your addiction, as we noted in the second chapter of this book. Here in Step Four you will see that your awareness of things, such as your creative ability, your feelings, even your relationship with yourself, was either exaggerated or diminished by addiction. It is time to begin to view who you are and what you are about. As you discover the difference between aloneness and loneliness, you will be able to work on acquiring the knowledge and support needed to maintain healthy solitude. We, the authors, would like to share with you our definitions of loneliness and aloneness. We see loneliness as a state of being with oneself that brings about negative feelings. These feelings are non-growth supporting. This state has an air about it of being thrust upon us rather than being chosen by us. The reasons for our loneliness are many and varied, and each of you reading this chapter can fill in your own blanks, but there are certain universal feelings that surround this state. Some of these feelings are separateness, sadness, melancholy, panic, depression, fear, stress, pain and lack of direction. Loneliness is capable of causing physical and mental illness. In contrast, aloneness or solitude is a sought-after state. It is energy producing and adds to rather than detracts from the quality of life. You feel good, revitalized and effective. In this atmosphere of aloneness, spirituality has a chance to work for you.

The opposite of developing a healthy solitude may well lead from alcoholism to workaholism, overeating, overresponsibility, even to compulsivity in recovery work. "A.A. is a way of life for me — not my whole life," responded one active A.A. member. "I need to get my life in balance and not substitute one excess for another," she went on to add.

Do you find yourself:
- Looking at a life that is out of balance?
- Substituting one dependency for another?
- Using your recovery program as a means to escape responsibility at home? At the office?

At first glance Step Four may seem to be almost overwhelming. The very idea of reviewing your life — of acknowledging moral successes and failures — may seem uncomfortable or even impossible. A woman in A.A. wrote, "With any gain I've achieved, which is quite a bit, I've always found the level of pain intense. To change takes power and faith that comes from my Higher Power. To acknowledge my inventory of both good and bad takes a strength that feels deeply spiritual." You have, in fact, already lived through your past, and now you can grow by making an honest appraisal or review of the events of your life.

As you did in Step Three, consider the specific words in Step Four. Take the word *fearless*. Fear is associated with emotions of alarm and anxiety in the face of danger. So the statement that you must make a *fearless* inventory is very appropriate, especially when aspects of your life may have been shameful, mean, or perhaps even cruel. (We will be addressing the issue of shame in Steps Five and Six.) One recovering woman said, "I have always thought of myself as a good mother, even when I was drinking. I had difficulty putting down on paper some of the things that I had done to my children during my active drinking days. Surprisingly, it was just as difficult writing down the things I had done that were good and beneficial for them. I had to rethink my definition of 'good' mother, 'bad' mother. Not an easy chore, but a necessary one." You must be courageous and brave, as well as honest and realistic. If you are going to grow spiritually, you need to be willing to examine and weigh the events and attributes of your life in as clear a light as possible. A part of this examination is to view in reality the strengths that you possess. Also, it is wise to cultivate a habit of acknowledging the work you do in maintaining constancy in your recovery.

An aspect of the fear and trepidation you may feel as you approach Step Four is a natural, normal reluctance to admit mistakes. But this hesitation is a stumbling block to the healing benefits of the step. "I found that some qualities I felt negative about just were, they weren't good or bad," one woman wrote. "I also began to prioritize relationships in my life — becoming more understanding and more empathetic." And, it will serve you well to touch base here with a sponsor or spiritual director in order to use this step as a foundation for building *sound relationships*.

Examine where you are with the following questions:

- When was the last time you called your sponsor?
- Are you being generous with yourself by listing your assets as well as your liabilities?
- Have you asked your Higher Power for help and guidance with this step?

It is important here to look at your "connectedness," that part of you that is joined in community with others. Women have many communities, home, work, political, and church, but just how connected are you to the people in these various groups? We have talked with you about developing a relationship with yourself — now is the time to look at the others in your daily existence. Which of these relationships do you need to reshape? A tendency might be to remove yourself from the unsupportive people and to find new associates. Try a different approach. Use your creativeness and work to reshape the relationships you have with others.

Reflect on the following:

- List the various communities of which you are a member.
- Are your relationships in these groups fulfilling and acknowledging to you?
- List the relationships that you would like to reshape or discontinue.

The second word to consider, *moral,* takes its meaning not so much from legal "rightness" or "wrongness," but from personal ethics. It is your conscience, your personal sense of right and wrong. Your conscience may be thought of as the "voice within that never lies." But you must listen with honesty and courage as well as with gentleness and patience if you are to hear and respond to this voice that is speaking within you. "My first Fourth Step experience was negative because I didn't want to accept my wrongs," one woman answered, "but as I opened my heart to my Higher Power, things began to fall into place."

Then there is the word *inventory*. At first you may be inclined to think of Step Four as a record of misdeeds or sins, but to do this is to miss the true meaning of the word inventory. The dictionary defines inventory as "a detailed list of things in one's view or possession" or "an evaluation or survey, as of personal characteristics or abilities." "Doing an inventory caused me to look at myself objectively for the first time," a respondent said. "It cleared away some of the 'junk' that had gone unattended for too long. It helped me celebrate my strengths."

It may be helpful to consider an inventory in ordinary, everyday terms. In bookkeeping or accounting, for example, you record both assets and liabilities in order to arrive at a balance. Including only the plus side or minus side of the ledger will not produce an accurate appraisal. A personal, moral inventory is a valuable part of life, and it will be most useful and complete if you are careful to include your strengths, your assets, as well as your shortcomings. A woman in Al-Anon wrote, "The most important things I learned in doing Step Four were that I have some real strengths, and that by awareness and acceptance I can learn to forgive myself and others. I also learned that some of my 'defects' were strengths misused." By understanding and recognizing your strengths *and* weaknesses, you will be better able to make necessary *adaptations in your feelings* and attitudes, and be better able to maintain sobriety.

Step Four is a developmental step, enabling you to look realistically at your life. As you take additional Fourth Steps in your recovery, you will begin to "compare yourself to yourself" and to acknowledge your own growth. "The last Fourth Step I did was thorough and honest," one woman wrote. "It was in a workbook for women alcoholics and codependents. It gave me an understanding of where I came from, helped me to have love and compassion for who I am, and showed me where I could make changes. I was able to forgive myself and start over."

Investigate your reactions to these questions:
- Are you afraid to take Step Four? Why?
- In what do you take pride?
- Can you forgive yourself?

A measuring stick that many women use when they are unhealthy is what others say about them, but Step Four allows you to develop self-esteem rather than to depend on the esteem of others. Lack of self-esteem is often rooted in a faulty understanding of what it is to be human. Recalling her early A.A. involvement, one woman commented, "At one of the first A.A. meetings I attended, the speaker said, 'Perfect human beings make mistakes.' I couldn't get that until little by little, it sank in — I associated not making mistakes with being good and now I know that there is no real association — just one that I had learned growing up." Just as this woman did, you need to rethink the positions that your family of origin passed on to you. Your *self-value* comes about when you are able to choose that which is important, moral and ethical for you. Chemical dependency untreated does not allow for you to select and adhere to the principles your inner self holds as truth. In recovery, you may experience the same uncertainty that an adolescent feels when she is combining all the influences in her life into a set of ethics that are a synthesis — a blend — that is healthy and appropriate for her. Allow yourself to go through this discernment. It is vital for your development. You will see the improvement in all the areas included in *self-value* when you have your own ethics to live by.

Pause again, and consider these questions:

- Is it okay for you to make mistakes?
- Are the ethics you live by your own or are they left over from the past and no longer serve you well?
- Are you able to accept yourself as the woman you are today?
- Are you able to feel good about the woman you are, even on a bad day?

The purpose of Step Four is to enable you to sweep clean your internal house and to open the door to the process of change. Step Four is vitally important to spiritual growth. It opens the way to self-knowledge and new awareness. With it, you can take charge of your life, implementing the changes necessary to move along on a healthy path.

Step Five Story

A mother coping with her son's AIDS diagnosis experiences a spiritual desert...

This has to be a sobriety story. I am too involved with what is going on in my life today to look too far back into the past. On the surface this may sound like it is as it should be, living in the moment, but if that is the case, it is only happening by circumstance. You see, I have a child, a twenty-nine-year-old boy — no — a man who is dying of AIDS. As his mother, a part of me is dying too.

When I thought about doing my story for this book, I thought I couldn't, mainly because this is a book about spirituality, and I am not sure where I am with this part of my A.A. program. I imagine most of the women who wrote for the authors had a positive message and a happy ending or at least a change of attitude to talk about. I have experienced all of these things in my almost sixteen years of sobriety. Some days even now, I feel that calmness, that serenity that is present when I am on a spiritual track that is comfortable for me. Other days when I can only think of my son and what is in store for him, I am not even sure that there is a Higher Power in my life. Other days, in desperation I call out to any power to help him — to cure him — to take away the pain. I guess this is what the books mean when they talk about "foxhole spirituality": Calling on the God of my understanding when the chips are down.

When I spoke with the authors and found that they were carrying a number of themes throughout the book and that one of these themes is to see the spiritual in everyday events, I thought I just might have something to say. I would like to tie my contribution to the Fifth Step.

When I was new to A.A., I took this step with a woman who was my sponsor at the time. I had made my list as suggested in Step Four, and I had prayed to my Higher Power about all that I had done. That part was fairly easy, but I was very frightened about admitting these "wrongs" to another human being. I took the plunge and it certainly gave me a new appreciation of this woman. She was attentive to me, she made sure I listed my assets as well as my liabilities, and most important, she was trustworthy and non-judgmental.

What does this have to do with my spirituality today? It was back there in those early days that a foundation was laid that was to take me out of my isolation. I began to take the risks necessary to have a full and creative life. Without such risk and creativity, I believe it would have been impossible for me to achieve any consistent sense of my own spirituality. It was this woman and all that she represented — the trust, the acceptance, the non-judgmental position she took — that was to allow me to begin to have supportive people in my life. People that help me to understand me. You see prior to working on Step Five, I was not capable of having a healthy relationship with anyone. My mother was an alcoholic so I had no one to teach me about what it meant to be a friend — a person who is around when there is pleasure and when there is pain. Then my own alcoholism robbed me of any chance I had of developing skills to choose people that were not as mixed up as I was. I now have that skill.

Since my son has been diagnosed as having AIDS, I have had to go back to some very basic things in every area of my life. Spirituality is no exception. I need to believe that God is not responsible for this disease and that He is sad too that my son is dying of such an awful illness. I have spent a whole lot of time reading and thinking about the God of my understanding and how these atrocities of life happen. For me, I believe this is all part of humanness and the design of this world — part of what it means to be in partnership with our Higher Power.

Daily, I have had to learn to accept the bias this disease brings out in people. To counter that, I have experienced an understanding and compassion from others I did not know existed. Daily, I see the hope fade from my son's eyes, only to see it return later in the day. Daily, I watch people that I thought would support me move out of my life because of ignorance, only to be replaced by others whose strength and support are unfailing. Finally, daily, I struggle to feel even the tiniest glimmer of faith and just when I am about to give up hope, I feel that connection to something outside of myself, in every fiber of my being. I need to end by saying that I am not sure that my spirituality is strong enough to remain with me throughout the rest of my son's illness, but I do know that it is here now as I write this and I need to be content with that.

Step Five

Admitted to God, to ourselves, and to another human being the exact nature of our wrongs.

No matter how thorough and honest you have been in taking Step Four, the actual reality of Step Five will probably awaken a certain amount of fear and anxiety. Admitting to God, to yourself, and especially to another human being the exact nature of your wrongs requires a great depth of personal vulnerability, and while this is a necessary step, you will do well to exercise caution and consideration in the working of Step Five. You need not rush into it. Your self-disclosures may be uncomfortable or embarrassing; they may be things you have never spoken about before — by telling another human being these things, you are entrusting a part of yourself to someone else. "I was ashamed and uncomfortable, even with my sponsor," one woman wrote, "because a lot of things I had to say were of a sexual nature. I chose to take my first Fifth Step with a woman who told us in a retreat that she had done some of the same things that I had done. She made me realize that I wasn't unique and that I wasn't disgusting — I was a drunk. I didn't have to do those things again."

Here we would like to share our feelings and understanding about guilt and shame. These things can and do separate us from both the human and the spiritual. Feelings of unworthiness always bring about alienation. When we either grow up with or move into adult relationships that are guilt and/or shame based, working on Step Five can get off to a rocky start.

Some say, "Shame is *I am a mistake,* while guilt is that *I make mistakes.*" This is fine as far as it goes, but we believe this minimizes a particularly prevalent condition women find themselves in. We prefer the definition found in *Shame, Guilt, and Alcoholism* by Ronald T. Potter-Efron, M.S.W., Ph.D. "Shame is 'a painful state of awareness of one's basic defectiveness as a human being' while guilt is 'a painful state of awareness that accompanies actual or contemplated violation of societal values and rules'." (pp. 1-2) One needs only to look at the liturgy of most if not all organized religions to see how feelings of shame and unworthiness are fostered and supported. This is an area in which we believe the feminine side of spirituality is making and will continue to make great impact.

Being shamed can produce devastating effects on your personality. Constant feelings of guilt about the past can intrude on your potentiality in the present. It is our hope that Step Five will help you to better deal with these two very human conditions.

Ask yourself:

- As a woman, how do you perceive shame? Guilt?
- Was your family of origin a shame-based family?
- Are any of your current relationships based on shame or guilt?
- Can you reshape these relationships into more healthy ones?

Take time to choose a trustworthy person to hear your Fifth Step: someone who can understand your discomfort and shame; someone who will listen without judging, but at the same time will be honest with you; someone who will not reject you, but who will see not only where you may have failed, but also your potential for strength and goodness.

But know too, that a part of the risk involved in Step Five is that the person you choose may not respond as you wish. One woman remembered, "I was surprised and hurt when I tried to tell part of my story to a friend. She had been very open with me about herself, but when I said the words 'incest survivor' about myself, her immediate response was that she could not listen anymore."

Most of the women who responded to the questionnaires for this book said that they had taken a Fifth Step with a sponsor. Others had gone to friends, spiritual directors, or therapists — there is no "best" person to hear your Fifth Step. Your Fifth Step may be taken totally with one person or partially with several people.

Pause for a few minutes and ask yourself these questions:

- Is there a "safe" person or persons with whom you can be open and vulnerable?
- Are you willing to risk sharing even a small part, if not all, of your past with another human being?
- If you have taken a Fifth Step was it a good experience for you?

No matter how uncomfortable the contemplation of Step Five may be, actually taking it has many benefits. Step Five, honestly acknowledging your shortcomings to your Higher Power, to yourself, and to another human being, provides opportunity for growth in spirituality — in *self-value, adaptability of feelings* and *sound relationships.*

One specific benefit of Step Five is greater objectivity and balanced perspective. The very act of speaking out loud to another person enables you to hear in a more objective way. Just talking about your wrongs or shortcomings takes away some of their power over you and releases the fear of secrecy and hiddenness. One member of A.A. recalled, "I felt such relief in telling someone else what I felt I had done wrong. I was given the opportunity to realize that I had made mistakes, but I am not my mistakes." Another woman said, "When I began my first Fifth Step, it was actually hard to say some words — they seemed to get stuck in my throat. When I finally did start to talk I could feel myself begin to relax, and that was a very freeing experience."

Take a break now, and ask yourself these questions:

- Are there secrets you have never told anyone, or even admitted to yourself and your Higher Power?
- Is there a word (or words) that has power over you so that it is uncomfortable even to say it aloud?

Another benefit of Step Five is an increasing openness and vulnerability, often leading to a growing trust of another as well as of yourself. Trust develops as you risk sharing a part of yourself with another, and find that you are met in return with respect, concern and even love. One long-time member of N.A. said, "In taking Step Five, I finally saw myself in the light of love. As I was more in touch with someone else's unconditional love for me, I began to feel forgiveness and care for myself." A relative newcomer to A.A. wrote, "For me, Step Five is an experience of acceptance, of being myself."

Although some women prefer to take a Fifth Step with someone they do not know, in order to insure their anonymity, many women wrote about the importance of the bond that develops in taking Step Five. "The experience of being forgiven, by God, but in the presence of my sponsor, was very powerful during my first Fifth Step," one member of A.A. wrote, "and has increased during subsequent Fifth Steps." And another woman wrote, "I was sure my Step Five was going to cost me a friendship, because I just couldn't believe anyone who knew the truth about me would want to be near me. What a wonderful surprise it was — I wasn't judged or rejected; in fact, we're still friends, years later."

While it is impossible to determine what the final outcome of a relationship will be after Fifth Step work, it is important to risk trusting another, knowing that even if your trust is misplaced, you will have grown stronger yourself for trusting.

Consider:
- How will you respond if another woman asks you to hear her Fifth Step?
- Is it more difficult for you to trust or to be trusted?

A third benefit of taking Step Five is a feeling of forgiveness and an increased ability to forgive others. Although the specific purpose or point of Step Five is honesty and healthy humility, forgiveness, reconciliation and a chance for a new beginning are important as well. A member of Al-Anon said, "Since taking Step Five, it's easier to forgive myself, and to trust that others will forgive me. It's easier to risk letting others know me." Another woman answered, "I've become less judgmental since taking Step Five, and I have a greater compassion for others."

How would you answer these questions:
- Are you able to forgive yourself? Others?

- Are you able to accept forgiveness?

One woman described Step Five as a "resting place." Step Five has a sense of completeness and summary about it, although, as with all of the other steps, you may choose to repeat Step Five many times. Taking a Fifth Step can "put to rest" your shortcomings of the past, and be a point of turning toward the future. By honestly admitting and acknowledging your past, you are able to let go of it and move into the future. One woman wrote of "knowing herself — owning herself" since taking Step Five.

There are times, too, when your best efforts at self-disclosure still are not complete — perhaps there are things hidden even from yourself that it is not time to know, or perhaps things that you cannot yet consciously admit to yourself or to your Higher Power. Remember, there is no "right" or "wrong" method with Step Five. Be gentle with yourself. Your psyche has a marvelous and healthy way to protect itself. It is extremely merciful even when we are not. Appreciate your accomplishments. Fifth Step work is difficult, but extremely rewarding. Working Step Five will deepen and strengthen your growing spirituality.

Step Six Story

A therapist benefits from intervention...

I didn't intentionally get sober. What alcoholic does? I couldn't imagine my future without alcohol in it. Drinking shaped most of my activities. The idea of never drinking again seemed a cruel, cosmic joke; and yet there was a tiny edge of relief at finally being able to name my problem. I blamed where I lived, who I was with, who had rejected me, the work I did and all the other external circumstances for my drinking. But in a dim glimmer of relief, I put my faith into giving this sobriety idea a chance.

It happened this way: I was employed as a drug and alcohol counselor in a large corporation. My colleagues performed an intervention, and I was given a chance to get myself into the rooms of A.A. and get sober or within ninety days go into a treatment center. If I couldn't get sober, I knew it meant the end of that job, and probably my career.

Faced with everything I understood intellectually about alcoholism, I had to admit that I knew a lot about the disease but nothing about getting sober. I sat in the A.A. rooms in awe of the people who were getting sober.

I am grateful to my first sponsor who took me to Step meetings and emphasized step work as a path to sobriety. She was passing along the gift her sponsor had given her and what had worked in helping her get sober. At first, sitting in the meetings, I felt completely crazy — nothing made sense. Slowly I began to comprehend how working each Step had made a difference in others' lives. As I listened week after week, and stayed sober, I saw the benefit of admitting my powerlessness. I opened my heart to the idea of something more powerful watching over the universe. I became willing to depend on this Higher Power. And gradually, I became willing to change my old behaviors.

Three years after getting sober, I left my counseling job and went into business for myself, a risk I can't imagine I would have taken in my drinking days. I've been blessed with a successful practice that has grown to a staff of five over a four-year period. Looking back I see how the wisdom of the Steps helped make this endeavor possible. When I became willing to let go of my insecurities and uncertainties, I learned to trust in myself, to believe that I am capable, and that I have something to offer. The Steps have given me the ability to include my inner wisdom "to thine own self be true."

Sobriety has also taught me the importance of using our God-given talents. I am a firm believer in pursuing the heart's inner passions — the passion for being alive. Surely the journey of recovery is about a continuous striving for a meaningful existence. Being on the spiritual path means staying in touch with what each can contribute, which ultimately is about becoming the best people we can be and sharing our gifts with others.

Step Six

Were entirely ready to have God remove all these defects of character.

The authors of *One Day at a Time in Al-Anon* refer to Step Six as "an inspiring challenge to surrender ourselves to the guidance of our Higher Power." And so it is, that having recognized and acknowledged your shortcomings and character defects in Steps Four and Five, the most logical next step is wanting your faults to be removed. That statement sounds simple at first, but unfortunately it is not that easy. "I didn't doubt for a minute that my Higher Power *could* take away my too quick temper," one woman said, "but I certainly wasn't entirely ready to let go of it — sure, it was uncomfortable sometimes, but my family just seemed to ignore everything but my yelling." At times like this, you need to make those around you aware of the fact that you are changing and you are no longer willing to achieve results with the same dysfunctional behavior.

Some shortcomings — defects of character as the Step says — are security blankets that, if only removed, will leave you empty and vulnerable. You will want to make a conscious effort to replace these shortcomings with other qualities. For example, sarcasm, which may be a form of humor for some, is often an expression of power and anger, so if this is one of your character defects, you will need to find another way to be powerful. One woman explained, "I use journal-writing to examine my shortcomings and to find alternative behaviors." As you begin to replace some of these negatives with positives, remember to substitute only those new behaviors that are enhancing to your quality of life, not just conduct that will please those around you. If it doesn't work for you, it doesn't work! Your self-value improves when what is changed adds to a positive perception of self.

Some character defects may be comfortably ingrained habits, or even enjoyable qualities. Character defects are seldom all "bad" — there is almost always a positive side about them, as well as their more negative aspects. The wife and mother who has to yell before her family responds, does in fact get a response.

Take a moment here to examine both the positive and the negative points of something you may think of as a defect of character — perfectionism. A number of women responding to the questionnaire admitted to struggling with this. Perfectionism is carried to excess for example, when you try to keep your home looking like a picture in a magazine, or you decide you must rewrite copy at work in its entirety when a little correction tape will take out the mistake, or you rip out an entire section of weaving for a flaw no one will ever notice. Negativity in this form stifles growth in spirituality and inner creativity and a possible relapse may result.

The positive side can be seen when, for example, you make sure all the bills go out in the mail when they are due, or you meet the project deadline at the office, or you can be counted on to arrive on time for a dinner engagement with friends. This is perfectionism's healthy side, the side that enhances your personal development.

Consider the following questions:

- Can you see a positive side to one of your shortcomings?
- Are the significant people in your life aware of the areas you are changing?
- Are you changing to make your life more functional or are you changing to please others?

With spiritual growth your shortcomings will become increasingly uncomfortable. Eventually you will come to the realization that further growth — in *self-value, adaptability of feelings* and *sound relationships* — can only occur if you become ready to let go of your character defects. One woman wrote, "I have recently discovered that I sometimes hang on to a shortcoming for dear life — like a pet worry, or people-pleasing. My struggle and my prayer usually are about *my willingness* to release my grasp."

Pause now and ask yourself:

- Which of your problem areas are most obvious to you at this time?

- Are the character defects you see at home the same — or different — than those you exhibit to the world "outside" your home?

Remember, the shortcomings that you see in *yourself* are the ones that you will want to have removed. While it is important to know what others think of you — how you "come across" to them — you are the one who must make the final decision about which character defects you want to have removed. A woman with many years in A.A. said, "First I have to recognize my shortcomings, then I can ask for help in working on them....recognizing them is the hard part." And another woman wrote, "I don't understand yet what all my shortcomings are, but as I become aware of them, I try to work on them with my Higher Power." Awareness is crucial here. Human nature, being what it is, does not appear to benefit from "other" awareness, defects brought to our attention by those around us. Maximum benefit is achieved when you discover what you want changed and then set about doing it.

Stop again and answer these questions for yourself:

- Which of your character defects interrupt your good feelings about yourself? About others?

- Which of your character defects stifle your ability to express your true feelings?

Although an immediate interpretation of character defects may be "shortcomings" or "faults," another understanding may be more helpful to you. Try thinking of character defects in terms of walls that interfere with your spiritual growth and hinder your development. Walls that shut you away from others and that close them out of your life are misused boundaries. By considering character defects in these terms you will be able to find the good in them, to emphasize their positive aspects while letting go of their more negative connotations. "The program has taught me to change the negative into positive," one member of A.A. wrote. Another woman said, "I either have to work toward removing my shortcomings or to find a way of better coping with them."

Usually, the walls that you create have served a positive purpose. Discovering that it is now time to remove the walls or at least to make doorways through them is not a matter for shame or embarrassment. Knowing and accepting are preliminary steps toward willingness to have adjustments made or walls removed, in order that *sound relationships* with others are possible. "At the beginning," one woman wrote, "I thought once I stopped drinking that everything would be wonderful and that would be *that*. But in the past two years, I've realized clearly it was just a *beginning*. I'll always have shortcomings and character defects — I'm human."

Another woman explained her willingness to have the character defects removed in this way: "I have learned to recognize in situations an opportunity to change my attitude or actions. Sometimes I ignore these opportunities and continue the old familiar actions. But when I have been willing to try new ways, I have been rewarded with positive feelings." In this way feelings are regulated by you and for you — they do not control you.

Consider for a moment:
- Can you see the walls that you have created?
- Do you believe that these walls serve to distance you from people?
- Are you willing to have your character defects removed? Some of them? All of them?

Step Six helps you to obtain spiritual wholeness by allowing you to become free from fear and paralyzing dysfunction, and to grow in *self-value* and recognition of self-worth. It means that you are not experiencing it perfectly. Step Six is the connection between Steps Five and Seven. It represents the willingness to continue on your spiritual journey.

Step Six is a "connection" step. It represents the willingness that *can* come only when you recognize and acknowledge your character defects, and *must* come if you are to ask your Higher Power to remove them.

Step Seven Story

A second-generation woman alcoholic talks about her spiritual discovery...

I grew up in a home with an alcoholic mother and a heavy-drinking father. Most of those years I spent taking care of my mother, doing her chores, pacifying my father and trying to make an abnormal home environment seem normal. The skills I learned during those years were survival skills that didn't work for me in situations outside my home. Distrustful of people and ashamed of my home environment, I became a loner. I was extremely shy and introverted. I was also prone to anxiety and panic attacks. I became a perfectionist in an effort to stay unnoticed. After all, if you were perfect, did everything right, made no mistakes, no one would talk about you or even see that you were there.

When I first picked up a drink, I couldn't believe how relaxed it made me feel. For once, I felt like everyone else, like I belonged in this world. It really felt great. I remember making a conscious decision to make drinking a part of my life. It was to remain so for thirteen years. In no way was I going to drink like my parents though. I was going to be responsible, get on with my life, and drink just to relax or in appropriate social situations. I didn't drink like my parents. I found my own style of drinking, one that put me on a slow but steady course downward into alcoholism.

At first everything was fine. I got a good job, met a nice guy, got married, and had two children. Gradually though, I turned more and more to alcohol to embellish, relax and fortify my days. Drinking became the most important thing in my life. With drinking came blackouts, hangovers, disgust, shame and depression. Certainly none of these things were expected or wanted.

By the time I reached out to A.A. for help, I was bankrupt in all areas, mental, physical and spiritual. A.A. saved my life and helped me put some order back into it. Every one of the Twelve Steps is carefully written and addresses a specific area for self-improvement and growth. I find it truly amazing how the theme of spirituality is subtly woven throughout these steps.

In each step, there has been some sentence, some phrase, or some group of words that took on special meaning, made me understand the step, and helped me to personalize it to fit my needs. When I understood the step and started to work it, I felt a quiet change in me, an increase in my sense of the spiritual.

Over the years, I had developed a strong reliance on myself — I didn't want or need anyone's help. I didn't want to be dependent on anybody because everyone that I had looked to for nurturing and support when I was growing up had failed me. It had become too painful, and I didn't want to be hurt anymore. Step Seven talks about "as long as we were convinced that we could live exclusively by our own individual strength" and "as long as we placed self-reliance first," we would have no success in building a faith and belief in a higher power. This bothered me because I wanted to believe.

The explanation of Step Seven goes on to talk about "the chief activator of our defects," as being self-centered fear — fear we would lose something we had or not get something we wanted. There was no question in my mind that fear ran my life. It had many facets — emotional pain, the unknown, people and failure, but what was this self-centered fear the step was addressing? I thought that the only reason I was riddled with fear was because of the way I grew up. What I came to realize was that I had also developed an arrogance — a feeling of disdain. Why ask for God's help or anyone else's for that matter? Where were they when I needed them before? But this step was talking about a change in our attitude, moving out of ourselves, asking for help, and a desire to "seek and do God's will." I became willing to make some changes.

It was not always easy to accept God's will for me — old habits die hard. At one time in my sobriety, about my seventh year, my daughter started to use drugs and alcohol. I hoped it was just a phase, brought about by peer pressure, but it wasn't. It didn't go away. It only got worse. Her drug and alcohol use totally disrupted our home and I became obsessed with the idea that I could somehow stop her and turn her life around. Fear took over my life again. I stopped going to A.A. meetings. How could I not be home to be the watchdog, the peacemaker, the enabler, the codependent? I stayed away from meetings for about three years, and I was struggling to keep myself together. I was totally cut off from any concept of spirituality, and completely removed from the support I had received from my friends in A.A. I did not drink, and I am forever grateful that I was able to maintain my sobriety. However, nothing changed at home and I realized that I needed to ask the God of my understanding for help for me and for my daughter, and I needed the strength of the A.A. fellowship.

For me, the spirituality of the Seventh Step is an awareness of the necessity to let go of fear and humbly move toward my Higher Power and others.

Step Seven

Humbly asked Him to remove our shortcomings.

Step Seven work consists of putting one's life in balance. You may choose to view your shortcomings as hindrances to healthy life function, and therefore of no benefit to a sober lifestyle. When you see these as something to discard because they are no longer useful, you can commence work on this step with enthusiasm.

Before fully addressing Step Seven, we would like to pause in order to do two things with you, our readers. First, we would like to explain the difference between humility and humiliation, and second, to share with you our working definition of humility.

A number of recovering women have told us their feelings on first hearing the word humility in connection with using a Twelve Step program.

Some of these uneasy feelings had to do with organized religion. One young woman expressed, "Oh, no! Here we go again: offer it up; don't complain. Don't think about yourself. Remember, there is always someone in the world who has it worse than you do. You need to be grateful for all that you have." Sound at all familiar? This is not humility. It is humiliation. *Webster's New Collegiate Dictionary* defines humiliation as "reduction to a lower position in one's own eyes or others' eyes. Extremely destructive to one's own self-respect or dignity." It may help to remind yourself that to be humble is not the same as to be humiliated. It means to be honest about your strengths and weaknesses. Even so, a whole lot of people believe that humility and humiliation are synonymous, the same.

The questionnaire that we sent out as part of our research for this book contains our working definition of humility. *Humility is an honest appraisal of our assets and liabilities combined with a willingness to change.* We believe this to be an empowering explanation.

Consider these questions:

- Does this definition permit you to look at humility in a different light?

- Do you agree with this definition or do you have one that suits you better?

Humility is a key ingredient in taking Step Seven. However, it is important to realize that merely asking your Higher Power to remove a shortcoming does not mean that something dramatic will happen all at once. Instead, this Step puts you in a frame of mind — in a position — that will, in time, allow your work already begun in the previous steps to be continued. This union between you and your Higher Power will allow for the removal of that which you choose to have removed.

Often, asking to have faults removed seems only to make you recognize a pattern of behavior that you can change. Asking for this removal may well adjust your perception of a present situation so that a way for you to change becomes clearly obvious. And while it might be great to fantasize that your Higher Power will "magically" remove your shortcomings, in reality this is usually not the case. One woman remarked, "When I become aware that some quality in me is adversely affecting my life, I ask God for help with that. It doesn't disappear instantly in most cases, but there is gradual, steady improvement. Sometimes the positive aspect of a particular quality increases as the negative decreases." Here again, as in Step Six, a partnership with your Higher Power exists.

Answer the following:

- Do you expect change without having to work for it?
- Are you satisfied with steady improvement rather than the "quick fix"?

Clearly though, asking to have your shortcomings removed is a way of growing spiritually — in *self-value,* in *adaptability of feelings,* and in *sound relationships.* It can help you grow by allowing good inner feelings. It can make you comfortable with the reasonable reactions you have to the *feelings* you experience. And your healthy "I" will join with others in *sound relationships.*

Asking to have your shortcomings removed is a positive statement of increasing *self-value.* You have honestly come to terms with a part of yourself that you do not particularly like and that does not serve you well, and you have become willing to let go of it. By asking for your Higher Power's help, you are affirming that you can change and that you are willing to work for change.

Most women indicated that the area where the most change was needed was their reaction to the feelings they experience on a daily basis. The desire for their *feelings* to fall somewhere in a comfortable range was extremely important. "Either I have no reaction to how I feel, or I rant and rave," said one woman. This is another area where balance is important. You will want to pause and examine the feelings you are having and consider just what a healthy response could be. You may want to ask someone you respect and admire just how they have learned to change unhealthy responses to healthy reactions.

Asking to have your shortcomings removed puts them in perspective. It is a freeing action too, indicating your trust in your Higher Power as well as your willingness to work creatively with that Power — willingness, as one woman said, "to do the footwork."

Consider these questions:
- Can you turn over to your Higher Power the freedom to remove your shortcomings?
- Are you willing to "do the footwork" involved in having your shortcomings removed?

You will also discover that asking your Higher Power to remove your shortcomings builds and enhances *sound relationships*. Several women wrote that when they had asked to have a shortcoming removed, they were more easily able to recognize an alternate behavior to replace the less appropriate one. Inevitably, this also has an effect on relationships with others. "I use Step Seven specifically to ask for help and guidance," one member of A.A. wrote, "and I have found a greater confidence that I will recognize and correct the shortcoming when a similar condition arises." As you meet situations with a new attitude others will respond in a new way to you. Your willingness to work this step and to participate actively with your Higher Power in adjusting your behavior will aid you in developing *sound relationships*.

Take a few minutes to think about:
- What relationship is most affected by a particular shortcoming of yours?
- How would a change in your behavior affect this relationship?
- Would you rather hold onto some of these unhealthy traits than ask for their removal?

Changing behaviors, releasing your grasp, humbly asking your Higher Power to remove your shortcomings, is an ongoing experience on your spiritual journey. "This is a process for me," a relative newcomer to A.A. stated. "First, I must be willing to let go of my shortcomings. Once I am able to emotionally release these shortcomings, I can pray with honesty, and slowly my shortcomings are being removed."

Chaos and crisis tend to remain when for whatever reason you chose to hang on to these pesky and sometimes extremely familiar faults. This Step effectively worked on gives you the freedom and opportunity to move forward in your recovery and spiritual growth.

Step Eight Story

An Episcopal nun shares her experience...

I am the adult child of two alcoholics. My father, a WWII Marine drill sergeant, came home from the war a changed man according to my grandfather. He had become an angry, foul-mouthed hard drinker. He also became addicted to Demerol and other pain killers.

My mother was a life-long depressive. She was suicidal and withdrawn. She didn't want children, and had no idea how to care for them. Most of her time was spent locked in a darkened bedroom with foil-covered windows, a blood-red rug and a black bedspread.

I was six when my brother was born, and from that time on I was the "mother" to my brother and to my sister who was a toddler. My mother had abdicated her role as parent and given that job to me. Some of my earliest memories are of changing diapers and burping babies. The one positive, nurturing person in my life, my grandmother, died when I was four years old. I believe that she is the one who gave me the love and acceptance that kept me from going under in my later growing-up years.

We made the first of many moves when I was seven years old. My father's drinking was by now totally out of control, and he began to physically abuse me. I was beaten, tied into bed, locked in a dark room, and some memories suggest that he at least attempted to abuse me sexually. One of my father's male cousins attempted to sexually abuse me that same year.

My mother never hit me, but she shunned me and verbally abused me. Her most common punishment was to just pretend that I didn't exist...she didn't look at me, speak to or about me, set my place at the table, or provide me with clean clothes. I got measles during one of these periods, and she placed a bucket by the bed, locked me in the room, and fed me and cleaned me up once a day.

I was forced to clean the house while my mother sat in a chair and watched me. I vividly recall her comments: "...that's not good enough. If you weren't so goddamn lazy you'd do a better job.... My God! You! Can't you do anything right? Damn you!...Sometimes I wonder why I didn't abort you..."

My parents were like one disturbed person in two bodies; they were completely enmeshed. They were the only ones in the family allowed to express emotions or opinions. I was beaten if I cried so I learned not to cry. I have also been called "Radar" because of my acute sensitivity to the feelings of the people around me. Remember, my very survival depended on knowing what my parents were thinking and feeling almost before they did.

I was the only introvert in a family of aggressive extroverts. I considered learning to read as the most important event in my life. Books were my window on the rest of the world, and were the way I was able to solve problems. I knew instinctively that the adults in my life were unreliable sources of information.

In the 60's I became a peace-nick, a flower child. Of course, my father, with his military background, hated everything I stood for. I was, and still am, a passionate believer in nonviolence. At this time, I began to drink. For a few years, I drank too much and too often, though I never lost control. Being in control had always meant safety to me, so I couldn't give that up. I knew I would end up a carbon copy of my mother, that I too could quickly become an alcoholic, if I didn't stop drinking. I knew I had to stop and I did.

I entered an Episcopal religious community ten years ago, and began to experience, for the first time in my life, genuine acceptance of myself as a person. My problem was that I could not see that my experiences as a child were still very much with me. My confessor/spiritual director began to try to convince me that I needed Al-Anon. I refused. After all, I was a Christian, a religious, an intelligent person with a degree in psychology — what did I need with Al-Anon? After being patient with me for a year, he told me that we would have no more conversations until I'd been to a meeting. I was furious! But I went. I cried through my entire first meeting.

Since that night I've learned that it's our secrets that eat us alive; that I have choices; that it is safe to be who I really am. I have learned to feel what I feel, and think what I think; to own myself, not sell out to the should's and ought's of others. I have come to realize that I am strong, and that who I am is more important than what I do. I've also learned that God is not a vengeful punishing parent in the sky who only loves the perfect, and that I am loved just as I am. Today is where life happens, and no matter what the future brings, I have what it takes to face it and not be overwhelmed.

It was a long time before I could take Step Eight, and even then it took weeks of preparation. I had to take a look at my part in the relationships that I had with others. How had I harmed these significant people in my life?

Willingness to make amends was another hurdle. My father had a very rigid and negative influence on my life. It was years before I felt able to forgive him or to forgive myself. I was estranged from my sister and my brother. While working on Step Eight I decided to write regular letters to them, but it was nearly two years before either of them responded.

Step Eight is a preparation step. It anticipates Step Nine. Without the benefits of Step Eight the remaining Steps would be nearly impossible.

Step Eight

Made a list of all persons we had harmed and became willing to make amends to them all.

Here again recovery requires willingness. Looking back over the steps already taken, you can see that one of the threads of recovery is willingness. When you took Step One you were willing to recognize that there is a problem to be dealt with; Step Two asks you to willingly accept the existing insanity in destructive behavior and to willingly see a Higher Power as the means whereby this sanity is restored; Step Three asks you to be open and willing to risk turning everything over to the care of this Higher Power. A whole lot of "willingness" going on here, don't you think?

Then you move to that infamous "I don't think I am ready for this" step, Step Four. Surely a very large dose of willingness is necessary to make a moral inventory of yourself. Without that ingredient, how could you possibly do what is needed to continue on this recovery path?

Step Five puts willingness on an even higher plane because it asks you to extend outward even further than before by including others in your life along with your Higher Power. Steps Six and Seven require again a willingness to step out from behind blind spots and to look at those things you believe need to be removed from your personality.

Step Eight is concerned with personal relationships. This concern causes you to face those attitudes and events in your life that have hurt or harmed others and to become willing to make amends as far as possible. This step combines what is necessary for women in recovery to experience: *self-value, adaptability of feelings,* and *sound relationships.*

Step Eight entails looking honestly not only at mistakes and hurtful acts, but also at your part in disagreements and misunderstandings. It includes what was neglected or omitted, as well as direct actions. "I started my list with everyone who had offended me," one woman wrote. "That was pretty easy. Then I listed everyone in whose presence I felt uncomfortable, people who made me feel inadequate or guilty. Finally, I listed myself." By its very nature Step Eight cannot be easy or comfortable. It may require reviewing painful events of the past; it will be possible only with a large measure of honesty and humility.

Step Eight aids you in learning to feel good about yourself. You see yourself as worthy, deserving of forgiveness from others and also capable of forgiving those who have harmed you. It is here that you are able to look at the people in your life. Do these people support you or can you sense that they do not have your best interests at heart? If there are non-supportive people in your life, you may want to ask yourself why and how you can change or eliminate those relationships. Healthy recovery and healthy spirituality is about questioning, about choices, and about change. Get people in your life who you can give to and who give back to you — relationships that support mutual development.

Stop for a minute to consider:

- Do you often characterize yourself as one who has low self-esteem?
- Name the people in your life who support your development.
- Do your friends give to you as well as take from you?
- Do you often feel that you don't "measure up" to your own standards?

While working on Step Eight there may be a tendency to leave your own name off of the list of those you have harmed. Remember to put it there. You cannot possibly go through the events of your life that led you into a recovery program without having done some damage to your own self-value.

Step Eight may also be thought of as a preliminary exercise for re-establishing *sound relationships* with others, of becoming willing to take the first steps toward reconciliation with your Higher Power, with yourself and with others. You may make some surprising discoveries when you answer these questions for yourself:

- Have you made the list this step suggests?
- Have you ignored your own needs?
- Have you ignored the needs of others?
- Who have you alienated with anger? With aggression? With silence?

One woman summarized her thinking through relationships in this way: "I spent weeks reflecting on relationships, knowing that I shared responsibility for their quality. I looked for three kinds of harm, and when something came to mind I listed it. Had I harmed this person *materially*: Had I borrowed without repaying, damaged property, or harmed others in any physical way? Had I done *moral* harm: Was there verbal abuse or gossip? Had I deliberately ignored birthdays or other special events? Had I done or said things to humiliate others or to damage their reputations or to make them feel guilty? Was there *spiritual* harm involved: Was I indifferent to others? Had I buried my talents? Was I ungrateful? Had I misrepresented God in an attempt to control the children in my life, using statements like 'God doesn't love little girls who act like that'?"

A direct outgrowth of working toward understanding and reconciliation with others is the realization that you are able to make changes in your life. Step Eight enables you to acknowledge past wrongs, but more importantly to opt for change and transformation. A new and greater *adaptability of feelings* becomes possible through work on Step Eight. Explore your feelings about these questions:
- Are you willing to forgive yourself? Others?
- Are you holding on to guilt?

Step Eight asks you to make a list of those persons you have harmed and to become willing to make amends to them. Not an end in itself, Step Eight points toward Step Nine. Step Eight allows you to take stock of the past as you look toward the future. One woman spoke of it this way, "I came to realize that Step Eight provides a way to truly let go of the past, to achieve a certain measure of closure and a boost to self-esteem. Step Eight enables us, in a very practical way, to work through our guilt and shame and to begin to forgive ourselves and others. And it renews our sense of integrity."

With your list of those harmed and a willingness to make amends to them all, you are now ready to begin work on Step Nine.

Step Nine Story

A long-time member of A.A. describes the ups and downs of sobriety...

I began drinking when I was seventeen years old because I did not know what else to do with my feelings of loneliness, frustration and rage. By the time I was twenty-eight years old, I had everything I thought I wanted — a husband I loved, three children, a house, a garden, etc., but I still drank. I drank straight from the bottle, late at night, and I felt a desperation and an isolation that I still find hard to describe.

One very bleak Monday in December, I called A.A. for help. I would like to say that I was immediately enchanted with A.A., but the truth is I wasn't. It took a while.

I am a stubborn person and a slow learner. I have come to value my way in A.A. because, while it takes me much thought and effort to understand and use the tools of the program, it has been time well spent. It took me nine months of listening, thinking, identifying and comparing before I became convinced that I was an alcoholic. It was then that I could let go of alcohol as a solution for my problems. I knew I needed something in its place to help me live and grow. I began to use the steps to see if I could figure out "How It Works." (Chapter Five of Alcoholics Anonymous*).*

During my twenty years of sobriety, I have had periods of peace as well as periods of deep depression and anxiety. I have had careless phases when I did little more than attend meetings and say a little prayer in the morning and at night. These periods of complacency have been a subtle foe. I feel distant, a dialog starts in my head and I lose my serenity. Fortunately, I have been able to go back to the steps and return to the basics. The steps can be shaped and used for my day-to-day problems, not just to keep me from drinking.

Step Nine helps me to be in reality. I must dispense with the use of fantasy to relieve my discomfort. It allows me the opportunity to look at my relationships with others. A big part of working Step Nine for me is learning to be still — the stillness that allows me to see exactly when and to whom I need to make amends. When I make the amends needed, my relationships with others become open and honest. I feel that I am with people rather than isolated from them.

Where am I spiritually after all this time in so-briety? Sometimes I'm filled with a stillness and a sense of unity and love while at other times I feel envy or self-pity. I question my progress when my defects show up. It is at these times I need to remember that my purpose is just to be the person my Higher Power intends me to be. I have just come out of six years where a whole lot of what I believe in was tested: sickness, deep family misunderstandings, job changes, children moving on, financial woes, anger at "the church," etc. I have not always handled these situations as well as I would have liked. Maybe I need to make amends to myself for expecting me to be more than human when things go wrong in my life. I believe that length of time in the program does not protect us from the problems of life. A.A. gives us the opportunity to accept life on life's terms and to stay sober while doing that.

Step Nine

Made direct amends to such people whenever possible, except when to do so would injure them or others.

The great majority of the respondents to our questionnaire reported that taking Step Nine had followed Step Eight in short order. Most of the women, having honestly recognized and named those whom they had injured or offended, were ready, if not eager, to make amends. Some women found the making of amends difficult: "I've tried many times," one member of N.A. reported, "sometimes I've been successful." Another wrote, "I've tried to make direct amends, but some people are out of my present life." For other women, making direct amends brought peace and joy. "I have made amends," one A.A. member said, "and have been surprised at the loving responses I have received."

In the discussion of Step Ten, we will explore the connection between making amends and asking for forgiveness, but here with Step Nine, consider how making direct amends can aid your spiritual growth — growth in *self-value,* in *adaptability of feelings,* and in *sound relationships.*

No matter how difficult or embarrassing you may imagine it will be to face those whom you have harmed, doing so will increase your own *self-value* and improve your *relationships* with others. Making amends takes courage and humility. You not only have to admit poor behavior, but may somehow want to attempt to make restitution for past mistakes. Whatever form your amend making takes, you will feel more positive about yourself for having tried to make an unhappy situation better.

And do not forget yourself in this step. Addictions also do physical, spiritual, mental and emotional harm to the dependent one, and you need to discover ways of making amends to yourself. You may have avoided exercise or good nutrition, neglected your appearance and self-care. It is important to make amends in these areas too. Throughout this book, we have placed considerable emphasis on taking care of yourself. We have done this because we believe that the majority of women in our society have difficulty in this area. The first thing you need to do is to come to believe that indeed this is not only valuable and necessary but an extremely healthy way to live life. It is only when the nurturer is nurtured that optimal quality of life exists.

Medical research has proven that moderate exercise is beneficial to all. Can you even with your busy schedule fit in an exercise class? What about a thirty-minute walk around your neighborhood? If not, you need to ask yourself, why not? Surely if the doctor told you that it was necessary for you to do either of these things for one of your children, you would find the time. Look at where you truly are with the concept of *self-value*.

How do you take care of your spiritual health? Do you create an atmosphere where you can be alone with your thoughts, a safe place for prayer and meditation? Do you allow time for the creative expression of yourself? This too is part of your emerging spirituality. Recall again that spirituality comes from within us.

What about your emotional well being? Do you know how you feel at any given moment or do you just say "I'm fine," without really thinking about how you are? Can you name your feelings? Remember when we spoke of naming in the beginning of this book. We believe that the naming and knowing of good feelings enables you to have a sense of your own legitimate power. At the same time, to name and to know your negative feelings denies them the power to control you. This further aids you in your ongoing process of learning how to *adapt your feelings* in a beneficial way to life's situations. After taking yourself into account, you will be better able to make amends to others.

In commenting on her need to make amends, one long-time member of A.A. said, "I feel that my drinking behavior had shortchanged me — I had lost friends and possible loving exchanges...amend making seems to open up the lock on my heart." She continued, "...withholding an amend just makes me more bitter than before." The elements of spirituality — *self-value, adaptability of feelings* and *sound relationships* — are always closely intertwined. Here, in Step Nine, you can see just how much related one to the other they are.

The second phrase of this step — "except when to do so would injure others" — is also an important one, and must not be minimized or forgotten. In close relationships, particularly with family and friends, it is possible that your amend making may needlessly re-open old wounds, recall another's failings, or imply blame or guilt of another. Take time to consider the implications of your amends and to word your statements in non-argumentative, non-judgmental ways. In your eagerness to be completely open and honest, and to make up for any past failings or faults, remember to be sensitive to the other person. It is extremely important for you to make amends to those whom you have harmed, but never at their further expense.

Ask yourself:

- Are there those on your Step Eight list who would be injured by your admissions to them?
- Will your making amends somehow draw another's actions or motives into question?

In cases when you are not able to make direct, personal amends, consider finding alternative methods. One woman spoke of her "continuing sobriety" as the best amend she could make to her children for the time they had lost with her.

You may wonder how to make amends to someone who is dead. One A.A. member told us, "I decided to make soup for the homeless shelter in my area. I committed myself to one day a week from September until March. This is how I told my Dad that I was sorry for all the pain I had caused him." You can get pretty creative if you take the time to think of beneficial ways to make amends when the direct way is closed to you.

Pause now and ask yourself:

- Are you included on the list of people you have harmed?
- Have you begun the amends making process as yet?

- Have you tried to think of creative ways to make indirect amends?

Regardless of how good you may feel when you are able to make amends, there will be times when you must forego this, and know only that your present and future conduct and behavior will serve as an ongoing amend for something in the past that you cannot make up.

After Step Nine you will have cleared away most of the troublesome things of the past. Moving forward to Step Ten and its suggested daily spot check will enable you to keep current with the amends making process.

Step Ten Story

A mother talks about the dailiness of spiritual growth...

I would like my story to begin with my sobriety. I came into A.A. twenty years ago and I have maintained continuous sobriety since then. I arrived with a belief in a Higher Power, whom I called God. That is all that it was though — a belief — not any kind of relationship. I would mind my own business and He could mind His. It is not hard to see that I was one angry lady in early sobriety. This anger stemmed from the fact that, during my active alcoholism, I had at various times asked God to remove this burden from me. He didn't, so He was on "my list" along with a whole lot of other people who had committed transgressions against me, either real or imagined. I believed I was justified feeling this way. I would take the responsibility for my behavior, and give it to someone else. This got me off the hook every time, or so I thought. All it really did was postpone my getting help.

This angry attitude toward God and toward almost everyone else who crossed my path, lasted some years into sobriety. Early in my recovery, *what I got from A.A. was the gradual ability to keep the anger from spilling over and affecting everyone around me. This was by far not the optimal way to handle anger, but remember twenty years ago, we were not as psychologically sophisticated as we are today. There were very few books written about alcoholism, certainly none like this one. If there were, most of us would not have wanted to go into a bookstore and buy them. We have seen a healthy attitude toward alcoholism and other addictions develop over these many years. This is due in part, to the fact that some people of notoriety have allowed us to see their humanness and shared their addiction as well as their recovery.*

I was in recovery for about two years before I would even begin to think about the steps that had the word God in them. After all, this was a program of suggestions, wasn't it? To me that meant that if I didn't want to take certain steps, I didn't have to. To be sure, I wasn't going to. I chuckle at my arrogance now. Here I had been given a most precious gift, the gift of sobriety, and I was, true to my old form, going to do it the way I wanted to do it. I believe that my Higher Power gives me this gift freely, with no strings attached. There were times when I almost returned it, but I didn't and I am grateful that I chose to stay with sobriety and the program.

My active involvement with my Higher Power actually began when I was four years sober. My mother was dying of cancer at the time, and I knew that it would please her if I went back to church. I was not capable of doing that, so I did what I thought was the next best thing. I went to a retreat given for women who were members of A.A. My mother died five weeks after that retreat.

I was raised Roman Catholic and that remains my organized religion of choice, but I am in a very different place today than I was ten or twenty years ago with regard to a personal relationship with a Higher Power. What I sought in "The Church" I have found in three places: in A.A., in church and within myself. I know who I am, and I know who God is in relationship to me. I have arrived at this very comfortable place today by using the Twelve Steps to guide my life. I have made, and will continue to make, many mistakes along the way, but the fact remains that today I am at peace with myself, with my reactions to events around me, and with the people in my life.

A very important step that continues to direct me along these lines is Step Ten. This daily inventory helps me to stay current. By that I mean it aids me in seeing what I have done well today, and what lessons I need to learn from the mistakes I have made. The perfectionist in me would like to be able to tell you that I never miss a day with this step, but that would not be true. I have finally gotten comfortable with things being a little less than flawless.

I heard at a meeting that the way one man begins his Tenth Step is to get into bed, pull up the covers and say, "Hi, God. It's me. How did we do today?" I like that. That is what I try to do. I see this Higher Power of mine as friend, maybe even colleague, rather than Father or Ruler. This is what is comfortable for me. In these two roles, I am able to ask for what I need and what I want, just as I would ask my friends or co-workers, rather than as I would ask a father because for me, there is fear attached to a father-figure. My history tells me that fathers are not very reliable. This works for me.

Step Ten, in a subtle way, aided me in giving up my need to do things perfectly. The ability to admit to doing wrong, at first only because I was afraid I would drink again if I didn't, allowed me to begin to know that nothing was going to happen to me if I didn't measure up to some standard. Usually this standard was vague and set by me, not the impor-

tant people in my life. *I have looked at this over the years, and I have come to the realization that the unrealistic ideals that I lived by were self-imposed. Part of my ability to take care of myself is to give myself the same room for error as I give others. Early in my sobriety, I would never have thought to admit that I had wronged myself, and that I needed to apologize to me. I might have stayed up well past bedtime to knit, sew or do needlepoint as a gift for a friend or family member. The next day I would be dragging myself around, still keeping up with my responsibilities, but never thinking I had cheated myself out of a good night's rest. Things have changed a lot since those early days. I now know that I need to take care of myself so that I am able to do what I want and need to do for the significant people in my life. I believe this is what the Tenth Step says to me when I read that I need to make an adequate appraisal of myself on a daily basis.*

The part of this step that I wish our founders had forgotten is that part which says "...and when we were wrong promptly admitted it." I would have been satisfied if the word "promptly" had somehow not found its way into print. Then I could have just played the waiting game — you know that one — if we wait long enough and avoid bringing the subject up, there is a very large chance that everyone involved will forget what happened. Or better yet, we can allow others to assume the burden of responsibility for what occurred.

It is still extremely difficult for me to admit promptly that I am wrong. At times, like A.A.'s Big Book says, I would like to "take the easier, softer way." I know this no longer works for me. A daily inventory gives me the opportunity to take an accounting of how I am doing with the process of turning my negative thought patterns and actions into positive ones. I need to ask myself, are the words that I use words that let others know that they have value just because of who they are? Or do people leave my presence and feel a little less cared for by what I have said to them? What do my actions say to those around me? Do I treat everyone with dignity or do I act as if they barely exist? I know that it is in these small ways that I can make my mark on society. I know that I will not make medical discoveries like Jonas Salk, nor change a country as did Gandhi. What I do know is that my Higher Power has given me certain talents that I am expected to use in order to leave this planet just a wee bit better than when I came into it. I know also that a way for me to keep a constant check on how I am doing in

constant check on how I am doing in these areas is
to maintain the discipline suggested in Step Ten.

Step Ten

Continued to take personal inventory and when we were
wrong, promptly admitted it.

Step Ten is different from Step Four, the other
inventory step. A major difference is that you are
encouraged to practice Step Ten on a daily basis,
and by that very nature the accounting is decidedly
brief. It is a scan of the events of the day. Step Four
asks you to be scrupulous as you delve into the
events that make up your own personal history and
to write these things down. Step Ten, on the other
hand, makes no such requirements. Step Ten addresses the spirituality of dailiness. Dailiness is
nourishing because of its reliability. Whatever your
routine is, work at home or office or both, it has a
comforting rhythm about it. This is what Step Ten
asks you to consider.

Working Step Ten does, however, require a
great deal of humility. As we explained in the discussion of Step Seven, humility and humiliation are
not the same. Again, humility is an honest appraisal

of our assets and liabilities combined with a willingness to change.

True humility includes a realization and an honest acknowledgment that you do have talents and giftedness, as well as faults and weaknesses. Certainly, none of us likes to admit when she is wrong. This admission conjures up all kinds of thoughts and anxieties. What if you are attacked after such an admission? What if you are laughed at? What if your motives and feelings are questioned? A woman with long-term sobriety wrote, "When I am fully accountable and responsible for my behavior, and I stop justifying what I have done, I am able to admit when I am wrong. It really doesn't matter what the other person does with my apology." "Making amends helps me forgive myself," another woman said, "I don't know if my family will ever forgive me, but that's okay." In other words your *self-value* need not be dependent on what other people think about or do with your prompt admission of what you have done wrong. Increasing *self-value* coupled with a daily inventory, reinforces a positive self-concept. An inventory taken, say at the end of the day, provides you with a way to check yourself out. What have you done with the day just past? Have you used it to your best advantage? This inventory demands truth and clarity in order to grant you the greatest benefit, so don't forget to list your positives as well as your negatives. Have you ever included as a positive the meal you presented to your family? Surely this is an act of spirituality to set forth the evening meal. Where do you list the trips to the pediatrician squeezed in between trips to soccer games, parent conferences and the like? Women tend to count as pluses only what they consider "big, important" things that *other* people do. We seem to spend a whole lot of time waiting to do something great. It is wonderful and marvelous to do what you do each day. Most things that you do are of a temporary nature such as the laundry, meal making, gardening, grocery shopping, etc. — how quickly the meal that took hours to prepare is consumed, the laundry is just put away and the clothes hamper is starting to fill up. What happened to the cross-stitch pillow you made for your daughter's first "big girl's" room? Feminist theologian Elizabeth Dodson Gray addresses this perishability of women's creativity in her book titled *Sacred Dimensions of Women's Experience:*

> Women's creativity is expressed in what is perishable, transitory, fleeting, ephemeral.

Women's creative impulses are invested in perishable foods, fleeting flower arrangements, sensitive relationships with people who grow old and die, in rearing children who grow up and go away.... Women's creativity is a different kind of spirituality. It is a valuing of the moment.... (p. 9)

When practiced on a daily basis, Step Ten permits you to handle today and not to carry it into tomorrow. You are taking care of yourself.

Deliberate on the following:

- Do you take an inventory of the day's events when you go to bed each night?
- Do you consider self-care in your daily inventory?
- Do you value the moment?
- Do you place spiritual value on routine events?
- Is this a new way for you to look at your spirituality?

Step Ten is a step that calls your attention to disciplining yourself. This refers to setting up a routine that will allow you to live a full life on a daily basis. It helps you to maintain a sense of stability in the way you handle your feelings and emotions. You are asked to keep yourself on an even keel and should you fail at that and act inappropriately, to check yourself out and take the appropriate action. Suppose you lose your temper at work and lash out at a co-worker. Can you truly be working a good program if you don't stop for a second and evaluate what has happened? Remember though, it is only necessary to take responsibility for what is yours. Everything is not always your fault. After this spot check, you can make amends and begin again to keep feelings and reactions at an appropriate level. "I was in N.A. a long time before I realized that I could start a new twenty-four hours any time I chose. Before I began to use Step Ten on a daily basis, I thought if I did something wrong at eight o'clock in the morning, my whole day was ruined. Now, I change what I need to and can start a whole new twenty-four hours at eight thirty," commented one woman. Step Ten enables you to maintain a sense of flexibility and willingness to adjust and adapt your feelings.

Review:

- Are you able to start your day over any time you choose or do you let a mistake ruin the whole day?
- Are you more able to regulate your feelings when you are mindful of what is going on inside you?

- Do you notice an increase in your ability to adapt your feelings appropriately even when those around you push your buttons?
- Can you sort out what belongs to you and what belongs to someone else?

There are many ways in which you can get off course. Early in sobriety you tend to work only on the most obvious faults. As you become more in tune with your recovery, as you grow spiritually, you realize that there are many not-so-obvious ways to miss the truth. With time, in the program, each of us learns that deep within resides an inner voice that always tells the truth. For example, have you ever come home from a meeting after neglecting to go over to the newcomer and give her your telephone number? Something inside just doesn't feel right. It is just a bit bothersome. Here is when Step Ten helps you put your finger on the root of the problem. It says that you may have been thoughtless or unkind. Something wasn't done. Your inner voice has sent out an alert. Here also, you are guided not to exaggerate what happened. Check out the mistake, acknowledge it and learn to change the offending behavior.

Sound relationships are one of the ultimate goals of all recovery. Faulty relationships occur in all areas: with a Higher Power, with yourself, with family and with friends. Twelve Step programs address the lack of skill in this area. "Since my husband and children were the ones I hurt," one woman wrote, "staying 'sober' on a daily basis has been the greatest amend I can give them...I have a better understanding of life itself — a better knowledge of myself and other people — which makes relationships a lot healthier."

Many women wrote of the connection between making amends and asking for forgiveness. One said, "Asking for forgiveness means asking to return to a right relationship with another."

Take a few minutes to consider:

- What relationships are difficult for you right now?
- What relationships are good for you right now?
- Is there a connection for you between making amends and asking for forgiveness? If so, what is the connection?

Working Step Ten on a daily basis is an integral part of your ongoing recovery. Step Ten provides stability and humility out of which creative change can grow. This step helps you maintain a sense of balance. Done on a daily basis, it keeps you from getting too far off of your healthy course of growth.

Step Eleven Story

A writer dealing with sexual abuse issues says...

Little by little, and though I cannot fully explain how or why, the past few years have brought vast changes in my spiritual life. Meditation and prayer have become vital elements of my everyday living, and as I seek to know my Higher Power, I have been drawn more and more into a kinship with Wisdom — Sophia, most feminine gift of the Holy Spirit.

I do know that a large part of my practice of meditation has grown through my participation in Al-Anon, and through work with a spiritual director who is a member of A.A. Ironically, I joined Al-Anon in an effort to better understand several of my co-workers who belong to A.A....none of them was actively drinking, but A.A. meetings and the Twelve Steps were important to them, and I really wanted to know what they were talking about.

However, a curious thing happened: as I listened to the others talking about recovery and Twelve Step work, I began to get in touch with my own feelings and thoughts — with pain and fear and secrets hidden in my life. I had been sexually abused as a child — caressed and cuddled and fondled inappropriately, both as an expression of caring love and as punishment. As a very young child I had been touched sexually in ways that felt good, and I had been touched sexually as punishment in ways that were painful. The abuse did stop, but by then I had learned to abuse myself in order to feel loved and cared for as well as to punish myself for real or imagined faults and mistakes.

Discovering Twelve Step programs was never in my plans — I would never have believed that my life had become unmanageable or that I was powerless over my compulsions about punishment, eating and sleeping. But I also never knew how to explain my explosive temper, or my overactive gagging reflex when anyone kissed me or touched my face, or my preoccupation with my body and weight, or by abuse of over-the-counter medications. However, my friends in A.A. and Al-Anon accepted me where I was, as I was, and I began to accept myself too. I entered therapy as a means of growing personally and spiritually. An A.A. friend talked to me for hours as I obsessed about hurting myself, empathetically assuring me that she too had felt such a struggle when giving up alcohol and cigarettes. And it was she who first encouraged me, in the middle of my pain and frustration, to turn to my Higher Power. Later, to increase and build my relationship with my Higher Power, she suggested specific periods of meditation and prayer.

Prayer and meditation were not new to me — I had read and studied Agnes Sanford's experiences with healing through prayer and had for a time been a member of a centering prayer group. I understood prayer best not only as conversation with my Higher Power, but also as intense, creative, directed energy. But now, I have begun to use prayer and meditation in a slightly different context. I am learning the possibilities for entrusting my Higher Power with situations I cannot control. I have stopped struggling to discover the faces of those who abused me, confident in my belief that I do not need to know who hurt me. I do know that my Higher Power wants me to be as healthy and strong as possible — and a part of that means not to abuse myself anymore.

Slowly and tentatively I began to search and study and listen to my Higher Power — to God as I understand God. Slowly at first, but now more strongly and vividly, I am discovering anew my spiritual journey.

Step Eleven

Sought through prayer and meditation to improve our conscious contact with God *as we understood Him,* praying only for knowledge of His will for us and the power to carry that out.

As we noted at the end of the previous chapter, Step Ten is a daily step, but your developing spirituality will need other exercises in addition to a personal inventory and prompt making of amends. And it is here, in Step Eleven, that you are given the specific suggestions of prayer and meditation. While it is surely beyond the scope of this book to attempt a full explanation or examination of the practice of prayer and meditation, we will share some very basic techniques that we have found helpful and that can be used regardless of varying concepts of a Higher Power.

It is important to remember that in prayer and meditation, as in any other learning activity or exercise, there will be difficult times — empty or "desert" times — as well as times full of joy and serenity. "Conscious" implies an awareness of both discomfort and happiness, you cannot have one fully without the other. Many women expressed strong feelings about these difficult times. "Sometimes I have no concept of what serenity is, I only get glimmers of it. One of the things I have gained in my group is knowing that it is all right that I don't have serenity all of the time; I don't feel that I am a failure," one woman wrote of her struggles. Another wrote, "to me joy is a complex thing — I've been wonderfully, brainlessly happy lots of times — but joy is deeper, quieter, fuller, wiser, and I can say that there are beautiful places even in the desert." And another: "I've learned not to fight the times when my mind seems blank and directionless. Sometimes I find listening to music helps — I'm not a musician, but the comforting effort of melody and harmony somehow re-orients me toward my Higher Power."

But what about some specific guidelines for prayer and meditation? In thinking of prayer as conversation or contact with a Higher Power, it may help to remember that there is more than simply asking for what you want or need for yourself or others. Prayer, whether you use formal, set words, or your own more informal expressions, includes praise, thanksgiving, and even acknowledgment of shortcomings. Also, as we, the authors, have suggested throughout this book, we hope you will place emphasis on what occurs on a daily basis. Your life as you live it day by day is in itself a prayer. What can be more rewarding for a woman than to see that all is spiritual — that all is prayerful — as we go about living life as it is given to us. While prayer may come almost naturally for some women, others find the very idea of meditation feels foreign or uncomfortable. "I feel inadequate because I can't meditate...I compare myself to others in this area. I'm sober long enough to know that I am where I'm supposed to be, but I wish I were somewhere else. I truly don't know what other people mean by 'meditation.' When I've tried picturing myself at a beach, there is always a bug on my blanket that distracts me," one member of A.A. said.

It is important to know that there is more than one kind of meditation — there is no "right" or "wrong" about it. Meditation involves stilling and quieting the body and the mind, and focusing all energy, thought and feeling on a single subject. Meditation is relaxing and at the same time, energizing. One kind of meditation involves concentration on a single word or phrase to the exclusion of everything else; another type of meditation uses guided imagery; another follows a carefully planned outline of thought. Answers to questions may come during meditation, or perhaps guidance about a particular course of action or direction. In the context of Step Eleven, a primary purpose of meditation is to *be* in the presence of your Higher Power, to discover for yourself the will of God as you understand God, and then, having learned that will, to gain the strength to carry it out. "I am becoming more in tune with God, my Higher Power," one young woman wrote, "learning to accept His will for me. I am changing some of my old attitudes toward a Higher Power." And a much older woman said, "I know that my Higher Power helps me — it has been proven to me so many times. My trouble sometimes is following His will for me and trying to carry it out — my will gets in the way."

Remember, too, no single type of meditation is best for everyone — in fact, a variety of meditative styles may be used by the same person at different times. Prayer and meditation are freeing, empowering activities — try several styles, find what is most comfortable and what works for you.

Pause now, and answer these questions for yourself:

- Do you have a conscious contact with your Higher Power?

- Do you make a time and place each day for prayer and meditation?
- What is your favorite form or type of meditation?
- On your spiritual journey have you experienced periods of emptiness as well as periods of spiritual peace?

But what does Step Eleven have to do with the theme that runs throughout this book? Practicing prayer and meditation is one means of enhancing *self-value, adaptability of feelings* and *sound relationships.*

We have chosen to write about meditation because, while most of us know some prayers and can pray, many of the women responding to our questionnaire wrote about difficulties with meditation. The greatest difficulty, often compounded by work and family responsibilities, was listed as finding the necessary time, place and solitude. But many women wrote about their lack of discipline as well. "Time *is* a problem," one member of A.A. responded, "but making yourself *take* the time is a bigger one...I'm not schedule-oriented in my private life." Another woman said simply, "I don't yet have a handle on meditation."

Meditation is one way of developing greater self-confidence and *self-value* by allowing us to relax and accept ourselves where we are. "Sometimes I judge myself as spiritually 'inactive' if I'm not participating in 'formal' prayer, when actually my faith is very deep and very much a part of me," one woman wrote. Meditation may well assist you in realizing that you are not only valuable for what you actively "do."

One type of meditation that is particularly useful in developing self-value is guided imagery. In this type of meditation let your mind take you to a favorite, peaceful place — the seashore or a mountain cabin, for example, and then allow your Higher Power to be present with you as you relax and become willing to share your innermost thoughts and feelings. It is also possible and often helpful to imagine that another person is present with you — "My mother was a good role model for me," one woman said, "sometimes when I'm not sure what to do, I imagine that she is present with me, and that helps me feel more confident within myself."

Take a few minutes to consider the following questions:

- What is *your* favorite peaceful place?
- What thoughts and feelings would you most like to share with your Higher Power today?
- Are you able to take peaceful, serene times for yourself?

Another area of growth through meditation and prayer is in *adaptability of feelings.* "Rebelliousness, fear, not letting go are problems for me," one woman wrote, "and when I am afraid, really afraid, I find it hard to feel God will come to me."

Meditation is an excellent tool to use for getting in touch with feelings by allowing yourself to settle and be still from within — centering meditation is particularly helpful here. In this type of meditation, still your mind and body as much as possible. Choose a word or phrase that is comfortable for you and in some way relates you to your Higher Power; repeat it, as a mantra, silently or in a soft voice concentrating all thought and energy on the word or phrase. Begin this meditation for brief periods, taking time for breaks as you need them. Remember, meditation is not an endurance test — it should make you feel more at peace and in control of your feelings. This kind of meditation has a very calming effect on the body and mind, and aids in concentration and emotional evenness that will foster *adaptability of feelings*.

Pause and answer these questions for yourself:
- What relaxation techniques do you use to still your body?
- What is a word or phrase that relates you to your Higher Power?

Finally, meditation can help you grow in *sound relationships* with others. Several women mentioned conflicts in their spirituality and in "real life" relationships. One said, "I have difficulty differentiating between being a doormat and being too aggressive, especially at work. I have to live in the corporate world which sometimes seems to conflict with my spirituality."

A meditation style that may well help with *sound relationships* is a picture or story meditation. The point of this type of meditation is to see and understand a situation from a particular point of view by imagining how a certain character might respond. Choose a familiar story and then imagine yourself in the role of one of the characters — what are your thoughts and feelings as another character? What does your Higher Power ask of you and want for you in this story situation? This kind of meditation frees you to observe yourself with others and will often provide insights into your own responses in "real life." Let your imagination soar — if you're a nature lover, take a bird's eye view of the beauty in the world!

Many women feel, too, that their Higher Power speaks not only directly or through situations, but also through other people. "I realize more and more that in order for the contact with my Higher Power to have meaning, I must listen to what my friends in A.A. say," wrote one long-time member of the program. Meditation can help us to be more open and ready to hear what others have to say.

How would you answer these questions:
- Are you able to be objective about your own life situations?
- How does your Higher Power come to you?

Step Eleven offers prayer and meditation as suggestions for improving your conscious contact with your Higher Power, and encourages you to pray for knowledge of your Higher Power's will and the ability to carry out that will. Knowing and co-operating with the will of a Higher Power are important aspects of spirituality and of continuing sobriety. "I believe that my Higher Power has led me to the place I am now," one member of A.A. wrote. She continued, "I feel as though I am praying throughout the day, but would really like to devote one part of the day to prayer and meditation." Another A.A. member, with long experience of meditation concluded, "I pray every morning and meditate every afternoon. It is a part of my lifestyle today. I know that my Higher Power is always with me and guides me in almost everything I do."

Prayer and meditation are life-long activities — they are not done "once and for all," but are developed slowly and gradually, over a long period of time. The suggestions of prayer and meditation presented in Step Eleven may lead into the spiritual awakening named in Step Twelve.

Step Twelve Story

A dually-addicted woman, with twenty years sobriety, carries the message...

I grew up in a very negative family — my parents were divorced. There was alcohol and prescription drug abuse, and no religion. We didn't attend church. There were mixed messages about social behavior — principles were stated, but no one actually lived them out.

When I was about eleven, I began praying and wanting to know God, even though I didn't attend church. I felt different from my friends because I was the only child in my school class who didn't have a father. Even then my way of handling serious emotional conflict was to get drunk. As I look back, I was willing to pay any price to feel that I was distracted from whatever was bothering me. The price I chose to pay was the beginning of alcoholism.

I started college and stopped; I got married and divorced. I drank myself out of work and couldn't maintain friendships. I began having blackouts and many accidental drug overdoses. As my drinking progressed I felt hopeless.

Finally, with the prodding of a medical doctor, I got sober. Soon I began attending A.A. meetings. I was still taking Valium, but after my first few meetings, I said to the psychiatrist that I wanted to go drug free. He told me that I couldn't make it, but I told him that I wanted a chance to do this, and I haven't had alcohol or other drugs since.

In the book Twelve Steps and Twelve Traditions *it says that at some point most of us come to know God, and call God by name. It was not long before I began to see that Alcoholics Anonymous is a spiritual program. I saw that people's lives were being changed — not just my own, but other people's — I saw them getting better. The spiritual awakening for me is that by staying sober and practicing the principles of the program, I've experienced an inner change.*

The spirit of Step Twelve, for me, has been the spirit of service, and of principles to live by. I attended meetings as a newcomer because I felt this spirit — I felt cared for, seen, and safe for the first time in my life. And I also sensed that people in A.A. were living by principles which I didn't yet understand. I had yearned for something of value all my life, and here it was, embodied in peoples' lives. I could see that there was more to sobriety than just not drinking.

As a self-centered alcoholic, the idea of service was entirely new to me, and for some time I saw the Twelfth Step simply in terms of helping other alcoholics get and stay sober. In the same way that sober members of A.A. extended their hands to me, I returned this gift by speaking with newcomers at meetings, by accompanying other A.A.'s to active alcoholics' homes, by staying with an alcoholic through withdrawal, by taking a drunk to detox, by volunteering at Intergroup. At first, something of my ego was invested in this; but slowly I began to experience a far deeper joy, that of desiring to give without concern for any return.

Carrying the message to other alcoholics through Twelve Step work, service at groups, and being a sponsor are still vital to me. But over time the message has evolved into something far more. Today I know things I never knew in early recovery. I know that true healing takes place, that God can do for us what we cannot do for ourselves. I know that I am not alone anymore and that in all areas of my life I can — with God's help and the support of A.A. — be useful and happy in ways I never dreamt of. This is the spiritual awakening. This is the world in which forgiveness, kindness, self-examination and being responsible, and being of service are guidelines.

It was only after I was sober for about ten years that I began to feel some integration in my life, a coming together of what I valued and how I wanted to live my life. I became active in my church and community. I answered what felt like a calling to work with children, especially homeless children. I saw that opportunities for more intimacy with friends were possible, as well as for the healing with my family. I married a nice man. My life has become increasingly quieter and more focused. Where it was once a conscious struggle to try and practice the principles of A.A. in all my affairs, it is now the way that works best for me and helps me to experience the joy of living.

Step Twelve

Having had a spiritual awakening as the result of these steps, we tried to carry this message to alcoholics, and to practice these principles in all our affairs.

The Twelfth Step, which A.A.'s Big Book calls the "twelfth suggestion," sums up what it is that you need to do in your day-to-day living. Ideally, a balance is struck whereby the parts of your life unite to create an inner pool of energy. Life is viewed and lived from a new perspective. You now take what you have learned in meeting rooms, from sponsors and from what you have read, out into the world around you. Will you make mistakes? You bet! But just as the architect has blueprints to refer to, so you have the steps to use as a frame of reference.

"Having had a spiritual awakening as a result of these steps" is often the forgotten part of Step Twelve. You want to get right in the "thick of things" and start to help others. But, if you have not nurtured yourself and attained a reasonable measure of mental, physical and spiritual health, how can you truly help another? You need to consider the beginning of this step carefully before going onto the next section. The step is broken down into three parts and each of them deserves attention.

First, what is this spiritual awakening you hear so much about? "Early in my sobriety," one woman responded, "I thought that a spiritual awakening would be a sudden thing — a bolt out of the blue, so to speak. I was disappointed for a time that this kind of happening was not to be mine. My awakening was slow and quiet. One day, I stopped to look back at my life only to discover that the 'spiritual stuff' was present; it had been for a long time."

A spiritual awakening links you to your Higher Power and celebrates your uniqueness. Events of this nature are different for each one, and it is only as an individual that you can assimilate and use these happenings for your own good and the good of others. What a boost to your self-esteem, self-confidence and self-value to realize that the Presence in your life has given you something "special," something that lets you know that you are valued.

Pause and consider:
- Do you acknowledge and celebrate your uniqueness?
- Have you recognized a spiritual awakening in you?
- Are you resisting this part of Step Twelve because it sounds too religious?

You only begin to tap into the well-spring of your abilities and creativity as you work your individual program. Striving each day for progress demands that you take the time to pause and make contact with your Higher Power to see not only where you are going, but also where you have been.

It is easy to see and measure progress in the things that you have given up such as drugs or alcohol. But how is this measured in terms of your relationships with others? "Carrying the message" of recovery to others is, in effect, sharing your "experience, strength and hope" in all ways and circumstances. Your own story, like the stories presented in this book, can be records not of failure, frustration and chemical dependency, but of success, encouragement and sobriety. You give others hope for recovery as you share yourself. Your method of carrying the message to others may be by attending meetings, listening to another's Fifth Step, taking someone else to a meeting, or listening on the telephone when another is in distress. The specific quotations and stories that we have included here are concrete examples of Twelve Step work in action. Each of these women has been willing to share openly a vital part of her recovery.

Passing the message of recovery on to another can be as simple as putting out your hand to help, or as profound as allowing others to see your most vulnerable self, as you meet them with humility and kindness. Twelve Step work builds *sound relationships*.

For example:
- Do you share your recovery story with other women?
- Do you treat everyone with dignity?
- Are you willing to go out of your way to work with newly recovering women?

Having become aware of your own personal spiritual awakening and willingly shared your hope for recovery with others, you are then met with taking the principles of your program into every aspect of your life. "Practicing the principles of the program in all your affairs" may not at first seem logical or necessary, if the purpose of a Twelve Step program is thought of only in terms of maintaining sobriety or overcoming a chemical dependency. Included in "all of your affairs" must be the self-care that is mentioned throughout this book: taking time for your own creative pursuits, getting sufficient exercise and rest, eating nutritionally balanced meals.

But it is not really possible to stop there. Just as your past behavior influenced the activities of your daily life, the steps you take in recovery must encompass all of your living — at home, at work and in the community. The principles of your program must influence not only your personal life, but also your interactions with family and friends.

"When I came into A.A.," one woman wrote, "I was in such trouble with my drinking and so focused in on it that all I hoped for was to *somehow* be able to stop. I had no idea of what would take place in my life. A.A. gave me not only freedom from alcohol but freedom from the emotional sickness of my mind and soul. The Twelve Steps are an incredible formula for right living. The Fellowship guided me through them and to a Higher Power."

One of the most difficult places to "practice these principles" is in your own home with those who are closest to you. The Twelfth Step addresses emotional sobriety for you and for those around you. "Sometimes I leave a meeting and it seems as if I forget all Twelve Steps when I open the door to my house. Nobody needs to do anything. I just don't give them the same acceptance as I do my group members. I just react," noted one A.A. woman.

All masks are down in your home with the important people in your life. You may have little regulation in your feelings. While you may temper your anger, intolerance and irritability with those outside your innermost circle, those special to you sometimes bear the brunt of feelings out of control. You need to consider the possibility of bringing the outside person inside.

Answer the following:
- Is the person you are at meetings the person you are at home?
- Is emotional sobriety part of your own being?
- Where do you have the most difficulty practicing these principles? Work? Home? Meetings?

Ultimately, the principles of the Twelve Steps will expand the areas of concern in your life even into care for the earth and the universe, for justice and for peace.

We, the authors, feel strongly about social concerns, and believe that all of us working together can make a difference. One of us has spent many volunteer hours working and counseling in a women's prison. Incarcerated women, many of them chemically dependent, have few, if any, opportunities for practical counseling and therapy. As one woman said, "Prison should not be called a 'correctional' system — it does nothing to correct, but only punishes." Regardless of how you may feel about the worthiness of imprisonment as punishment, the failure of the system to address the underlying problems of chemical dependence, inadequate education and health care, and the emotional traumas of incest and other abuse, must concern us as women. The other author counsels women and men recovering from addictions, child sexual abuse, incest and eating disorders, with a special interest in the child sexual abuse issues. We both are of the opinion that when our society is looked at in the historical perspective, we shall be judged and judged harshly because of our disregard of the well-being of our children.

We encourage you to discover and develop your special interest areas. Women working together can make a difference!

In a letter written in 1966, Bill W. summarized the far-reaching purpose of all recovery programs: "The chief purpose of A.A. is sobriety. We all realize that without sobriety we have nothing.... [But] A.A.'s Twelfth Step urges that we 'practice these principles in all our affairs.' We are not living just to be sober, we are living to learn, to serve and to love." (*As Bill Sees It*, p. 94)

Our understanding of the fullness of Step Twelve is that you first take care of your own recovery by working the steps in your life so that you develop your own sense of spirituality. Secondly, you reach out to others who suffer in the same way. Finally, you take all of this outside of the recovery arena and into the world.

Summary

In the beginning of this book we invited you to join and share in a journey — to discover and grow in your own spirituality, in your ability to believe and trust in a Power greater than yourself. We have encouraged you to grow, as we too continue to grow, in self-understanding and in relationships with others. We suggested that you would not have to go far to find spirituality. It is right in the dailiness of your life. We have tried not to mask religion under the guise of spirituality. We have sought to show that this journey is ever-changing and can accommodate each of us on an individual basis. Your spirituality need not be ours nor the match of anyone's story that has appeared in this book. Celebrate your uniqueness! Make no excuses for your beliefs.

Throughout the book we have developed three common themes of spirituality: *self-value, adaptability of feelings* and *sound relationships*. We hope that as you try to enhance your present spiritual concepts, you too will see how important to your internal energy, creativity and development these three themes are.

Many women participated in our survey, lending their experiences and thoughts to our own, and providing us with a great abundance of insight. We have incorporated some of their quotations and ideas in every chapter. Other women, twelve of them, have shared their stories with us and have permitted us, in turn, to re-tell them to you. To these women we are especially grateful. All have faced a spiritual crisis; some, like the woman whose son is dying from AIDS, still feel on shaky ground with their Higher Power. Wherever they are on their journeys, they wanted to share with you, the reader, the specialness of their individual experience. Thank you all.

Appendix

Please check all answers that apply in any question.

1. Membership in which Twelve Step Program:

_____AA _____ACOA _____OA _____GA

_____NA _____EA _____Al-Anon

_____other:_____

2. Number of years in program:

_____1-5 _____6-10 _____11+

3. Age:

_____21-29 _____30-39 _____40-49

_____50-59 _____60+

4. Race/Ethnic Origin:

_____Native American _____Asian _____Hispanic

_____Black _____Caucasian

5. As a child, did you live with:

_____mother only _____father only _____mother and father

_____grandmother _____grandfather

_____step-mother _____step-father

_____foster parents _____adoptive parents

_____multiple caretakers _____other:_____

6. Do/Did you have:

____older sister(s)   ____younger sister(s)

____older brother(s)   ____younger brother(s)

7. In elementary school did you attend:

____public school   ____parochial school

____other religious school ____private school

____other:_____

8. In high school did you attend:

____public school   ____parochial school

____other religious school ____private school

____other:_____

9. College degree(s) attained:

____Associate   ____BA/BS

____Masters   ____Doctorate

10. Religious participation in childhood:

____Roman Catholic   ____Orthodox   ____Jewish

____Protestant   ____Buddhist   ____Muslim

____Jehovah's Witness ____none

____other:_____

11. Present religious preference:

_____Roman Catholic   _____Orthodox   _____Jewish

_____Protestant   _____Buddhist   _____Muslim

_____Jehovah's Witness   _____agnostic   _____atheist

_____other:_____

12. Current attendance at religious services:

_____never   _____daily   _____weekly

_____monthly   _____occasionally

13. Current sexual orientation:

_____heterosexual   _____homosexual   _____bisexual

14. Important practices/aspects of your spirituality:

_____meditation   _____private prayer

_____corporate prayer/worship   _____reading

_____music/art/drama   _____retreats

_____spiritual director/mentor

_____other:_____

15. Have you taken Step 4:   _____yes   _____no

16. Have you taken Step 5:   _____yes   _____no

17. If you answered yes to either of the above questions, were these steps:

_____nearly impossible

_____somewhat difficult

_____not difficult

18. How helpful is the Serenity Prayer to you:

_____very helpful

_____somewhat helpful

_____not helpful at all

19. How many meetings do you usually attend each week: _____

20. How important is Step 10 to your spiritual growth:

_____very helpful

_____somewhat helpful

_____not helpful at all

21. Are you:

_____married   _____single   _____separated

_____divorced   _____living with a significant other

_____member of a religious community

22. How much "willingness" was required of you in the taking of Step 3:

_____none   _____a little   _____a lot

23. Have you found that the effectiveness of your whole program depends on how well you work on Step 3:

_____yes   _____no   _____not sure

24. Was it necessary for you to take the Steps in order:

_____yes   _____no

25. Who or what is your Higher Power:

_____God   _____Allah

_____Yahweh   _____the Group

_____other:_____

26. How important is/was your sponsor in your spiritual development:

_____very important

_____somewhat important

_____not important

27. Do you have a spiritual director:

_____yes   _____no, but did in the past   _____no

28. If so, how often you consult with him/her:

_____weekly   _____monthly   _____every 6 months

_____other:_____

29. Was your Fourth Step experience:

_____positive   _____negative

Comments:

30. Did you list your assets along with your liabilities when you took Step 4:

_____yes   _____no

31. After taking Step 4, did you have a better understanding of your need to change in order to maintain sobriety/your program's goal:

_____yes   _____no

Comments:

32. List three fruits of your taking Step 4:

    1.

    2.

    3.

33. Since working on Step 4, have you been able to form a true relationship with another human being:

_____yes   _____no   _____not yet

Comments:

34. In looking back, do you feel that before you entered a Twelve Step program, you were dominated by others:

_____yes   _____no

Comments:

35. In looking back, do you feel that before you entered a Twelve Step program, you were too dependent on others:

_____yes   _____no

Comments:

36. Have you relapsed:

_____yes   _____no

37. If so, how many times: _____

38. Have you relapsed since taking Step 4:

_____yes   _____no

39. If you have taken Step 5, did you take it with:

_____sponsor   _____friend

_____therapist   _____spiritual director

_____other:_____

40. Have you relapsed since taking Step 5:

_____yes   _____no

41. Since taking Step 5, have you felt able to receive forgiveness and/or to forgive:

_____yes   _____no

Comments:

42. Is anger a troublesome character defect for you:

_____yes   _____no

Comments:

43. Do you take the inventory of others:

_____yes   _____no

Comments:

44. Are envy and/or jealousy recurring problems for you:

_____yes   _____no

Comments:

45. Do you procrastinate:

_____yes   _____no   _____sometimes

46. Do you set yearly program goals for yourself:

_____yes   _____no

47. Do you believe, as stated in Step 7, that without some degree of humility no alcoholic can stay sober (adapt to your own program):

_____yes   _____no

Comments:

48. Do you believe that in order to keep what you have, it is necessary to give it away:

_____yes   _____no

Comments:

.

49. Were you ever hospitalized in a detoxification unit or other unit applicable to your particular disease or disorder:

_____yes   _____no   _____does not apply

50. Were you ever in a rehabilitation or treatment center applicable to your particular disease or disorder:

_____yes   _____no   _____does not apply

51. Do you use nicotine:

_____yes   _____no

How many cigarettes per day:

_____other:_____

52. Do you drink caffeine:

_____yes   _____no

How much per day:_____

53. Do you believe that honesty, tolerance and true love of others and God are the daily tasks of living:

_____yes   _____no

Comments:

54. Have all the "Promises" of the program come true for you:

_____all   _____some   _____none

55. Do you take a personal inventory:

_____once a day   _____once a week

_____once a month   _____never

_____other:_____

56. Do you have a sponsor:

_____yes   _____no   _____no, but did in the past

57. Do you sponsor people in your program:

_____yes   _____no

If so, how many:_____

58. Spiritual growth requires change. How is your spirituality changing:

59. Feelings of understanding, healing, joy and community are indicative of a Higher Power's presence in our lives. Has this been your experience:

60. What is your greatest problem with spirituality (i.e., time to pray, study and meditate? spirituality doesn't translate into real life situations? etc.):

61. Have you asked your Higher Power to remove your shortcomings:

_____yes   _____no

Explain how this Step works in your life:

62. Does the following definition of humility apply to your own life: an honest appraisal of our assets and liabilities combined with a willingness to change.

63. Are you comfortable talking about your spirituality:

_____yes   _____no

Comments:

64. Have you made a list of all the people you had harmed:

_____yes   _____no

65. Have you made direct amends wherever possible:

_____yes   _____no

66. Is there a connection for you between making amends and asking forgiveness:

_____yes   _____no

Comments:

67. Do you have a conscious contact with a Higher Power:

_____yes   _____no

Comments:

68. Does this conscious contact constantly change:

_____yes _____no

How:

69. Do you use the Prayer of St. Francis as suggested in Step 11:

_____yes _____no

70. On your spiritual journey have you experienced periods of spiritual emptiness as well as periods of spiritual peace:

_____yes _____no

Comments:

71. Have you found the joy of living as described in the Twelve Steps? Explain:

Index

Printed in the United States
53282LVS00001B/43-90

9 780595 006359